WITHDRAWN

COMMUNIST CHINA'S CRUSADE

Other books by Guy Wint

INDIA AND DEMOCRACY (*with Sir George Schuster*)
THE BRITISH IN ASIA
WHAT HAPPENED IN KOREA
SPOTLIGHT ON ASIA
MIDDLE EAST CRISIS (*with Peter Calvocoressi*)
COMMON SENSE ABOUT CHINA

GUY WINT

COMMUNIST CHINA'S CRUSADE

*Mao's Road to Power and the New
Campaign for World Revolution*

FREDERICK A. PRAEGER, *Publishers*
New York • Washington • London

FREDERICK A. PRAEGER, *Publishers*
111 Fourth Avenue, New York 3, N.Y., U.S.A.
77-79 Charlotte Street, London W.1, England

Published in the United States of America in 1965
by Frederick A. Praeger, Inc., Publishers

Library of Congress Catalog Card Number: 64-22934

This book is Number 153 in the series of
Praeger Publications in Russian History and World Communism

The first four chapters of this book were originally
published in 1958 under the title *Dragon and Sickle*.
They have been revised and expanded for the present volume.

The text was completed at the time of the fall of Khrushchev.
It was not possible to take into account events that occurred
since the end of October, 1964.

Printed in the United States of America

CONTENTS 76499

	Introduction	1
1	Moscow and Asia	4
2	The Chinese Communist Party: First Phase	13
3	The Chinese Communist Party: Second Phase	28
4	Imitating China	47
5	The New Asian Power	67
6	Peking Shows Its Strength	83
7	The New Apostle of Communism	103
	Conclusion	122
	Appendix	125
	Notes	128
	Reading List	130
	Index	133
	Maps	
	China, 1926-37	26
	Contemporary Asia	50-1

Introduction

THE greatest ambition for communism in our time was to over-run western Europe; and for a few years at the end of the war it seemed to have a prospect of doing so. The opportunity passed away, at least for the present. But instead of western Europe, communism took control of China, with its 700 million people and its strategic position as a springboard from which to move further forward in Asia.

This has given communism a position of great strength: one from which it might hope to lay siege to the rest of the world, instead of, as in the past, being besieged by the world.

Together, Russia and China have enormous resources. Being contiguous and guarding each other's rear, they formed, as long as they did not quarrel, an almost invulnerable communist enclave. But during the past five years they have quarrelled bitterly, and the extent of the dispute is still a subject of surmise. At least it can be said that it is the most important event in the communist world since communism came to power in China.

It is a mistake to think that the seizure of power in China by communism was the result of Russian planning, or that it was brought about by a skilful Russian strategy. Though at first it proved of much benefit to Russia, Russia did not plan it, at least in the final and successful phases; and there is evidence that some long-sighted Russians were distinctly apprehensive of the consequences to Russia of its gaining such a mighty ally.

It is also mistaken to suppose that, throughout its history, the communist government in Russia strove ceaselessly to promote the advance of communism in Asia. For long periods it was remarkably indifferent. In the 1920s, it is true, Moscow had believed that a revolution was imminent in China. It recalled Lenin's prophetic remark that the road to revolution in London and Paris lay through Calcutta and Shanghai.* It intervened in Chinese politics. This was the period of Borodin and of Moscow's policy of guiding the infant Chinese Communist Party into an alliance with the Kuomintang. But this venture ended in one of the most humiliating and apparently complete defeats suffered by Russia. Once disappointed, Moscow—except for a handful of its China experts—became obstinately sceptical. Throughout Hitler's war, Stalin undervalued the Chinese communists, and believed that they had no chance of becoming the Chinese government. Russia gave them little more than token aid. Stalin thought that the realistic policy was to recognise, and then to blackmail, the Kuomintang. When in the post-war years Mao Tse-tung shot like a meteor to power, nobody was more surprised than Stalin.

Because the Chinese were left latterly to make their own revolution, unsupervised by Moscow, their tactics were home-made. They seized power by a strategy completely different from that used by the bolshevists in Russia in 1917. But as it had been laid down that communist revolution

* It has to be said, however, that this remark, though often attributed to Lenin, has never been located in his writings.

2

everywhere should follow a uniform pattern, they were embarrassed by this and tried to conceal it as far as they could.

Chinese history in the short period of fifty years has undergone extraordinary vicissitudes. China, from being a great inert empire of the archaic pattern, has moved to become today a highly organised modern power which aspires to lead the forces of revolution throughout the world. The process has been dominated by the figure of Mao Tse-tung, whose career and whose quality as an experimentalist in political institutions summarise what has happened in China in this period.

This book is chiefly about how communism came to power in China, and about the relations of Russia and the Chinese Communist Party. The mistakes, the bad advice, the misinterpretation and the Chinese party's eventual solutions of its own problems single-handed are one of the most curious chapters of recent Asian history. The book describes also how the Chinese model of revolution has influenced the rest of Asia, and the prospect it has opened up in Africa and Latin America. It is a book exclusively about the seizure of power. Communist revolution is of interest in countless other ways; but these ways are not the subject matter of what follows.

I

Moscow and Asia

IMMEDIATELY after the bolshevik revolution in Russia, it was natural that its leaders should be attracted towards Asia. They were driven by circumstances and their own theories. They held that revolution anywhere must either lead to world revolution or else be suppressed by counter-revolution organised by neighbouring powers. Therefore, as soon as they had seized power in Russia, they turned their eyes outwards, watching for their example to be followed, aiding and inciting the communist parties abroad. In particular they watched Europe, but some placed their hopes in Asia.

In any case, Asia must have attracted the Soviet Communist Party. The continent of Asia lies at the back door of Russia; and communist leaders working from Russia must have been fascinated by the possibility of organising for communism the uncounted masses of the Asian territories, whose domestic circumstances might seem likely to make them particularly susceptible to communist appeal.

If the leaders in Moscow were attracted to Asia as com-

4

munists, this was reinforced by Asia's appeal to them as heirs of the Russian imperial tradition. In Asia, the tsars had conquered an empire of eight and a half million square miles. From early days of Russian history, long before communism, many Russian publicists and thinkers had argued that Russia's destiny lay in Asia at least as much as in the West. This was a continuous thread in Russian thought. Some Russians have always been dazzled by the idea that, if the great land masses of the Eurasian continent could be united under one authority, the rest of the world would in the end lie helpless before it.

After the revolution of 1917, Moscow, surveying the prospects in Asia, could well think the times propitious to it. Especially it saw China, where the Manchu dynasty had collapsed and where provincial warlords had seized the succession: a China which was weak, divided, misgoverned, in agony, its society convulsed by the impact of the West, and therefore potentially hostile to the West.

That was clear to even superficial examination. A deeper vision showed prospects even more encouraging to revolutionary conspiracy. China, like the other old societies of Asia, was doomed to change and disintegrate as the result of the contacts with the West; and the next generation, in all classes, would be exposed to every kind of vicissitude. Amid the breakdown of religions, custom and traditional authority, communism would seek to offer the prospect of a restoration of order, authority and dogma; it would offer the hope of rapid economic advance, especially industrialisation, giving to the peoples of Asia the sense of power which in the first half of this century they so pitifully lacked. Communism might prove to be a crutch to carry the wounded youth of Asia over into the modern world. Communists could at least hope that their doctrines and remedies, so much cruder than those of liberal society, would appeal more than liberalism to a generation which was near to desperation.

5

These prospects for communism in China at that time seemed so glittering that Moscow might have been expected to drop its less hopeful enterprises elsewhere, and to concentrate upon Asia. It did not do so for a number of reasons. One of them was that many of the Russian leaders continued to be westerners by temperament. Their eyes were fixed on Europe; they found Asian revolutionary movements chiefly significant because they might be weapons for attacking the western powers by promoting disorder in their dependencies or spheres of interest. They would only try to promote revolution in Asia for its own sake when the prospects of revolution in Europe had faded. Another reason was a legacy of marxist thought. Marx himself had been pessimistic about the development of society in Asia. His views about Asia were ambiguous, but at least at times he argued that Asian society would not necessarily follow in the same pattern as western. He feared that a revolution in Asia would degenerate into the setting up of a stagnant bureaucratic and military tyranny which might in the end stifle the revolution in the West. Evidently he preferred to turn his back on Asia and put his faith in Europe.

The inhibitions in Moscow at first prevented a continuous all-out endeavour in Asia. But it did not stop the intermittent efforts, and in these the problem for Russian communism in Asia was where to find the handle for political action, so that the potentially revolutionary situation there could be used for creating a communist Asia.

For a brief period, it seemed that the means might be full-scale military intervention. Some of the leaders in Moscow were carried away by the success of the Red Army in invading Poland in the summer of 1920. Might not the Red Army over-run the contiguous lands in Asia, carrying communism with it as the armies of the French revolutionists had carried the revolutionary ideas through Europe? Some of the Russian tsars had had the same vision of Russian armies storming across Asia. In this early period of the revolution, direct military force was used in overthrowing the non-communist governments which had established themselves in parts of the former tsarist empire in Asia, such as in the khanates of Khiva and Bokhara. It was used in border countries, as in Outer Mongolia. Why not still further afield?

But subtler ways soon suggested themselves. The communist leaders realised that in Asia it would be necessary to call on domestic forces able to make communist revolution; military intervention from outside might supplement these, but the decisive thing would be the initiative in Asia itself. The Russian strategy would be to stimulate and direct these forces.

By this plan, communist parties in Asia would fight their own battles and ultimately seize the government in their countries. Moscow does not seem to have doubted that these revolutionary efforts would succeed in any country when the time for revolution was ripe, and when such a revolutionary situation coincided with the rise of a communist leadership able to turn it to account. It held a theoretical, not a romantic, view of revolution. Revolution was thus thought of as a matter for local action and for history. But the Russians were not so disinterested as to leave its organisation entirely either to the local leaders or to time. The efforts of the local parties were to be scrutinised from Moscow, their theories criticised, their energies stimulated. In countries which were contiguous to Russia, and therefore accessible, Russian intervention could be more direct. Communism in Asia was in these days an international movement whose supreme, if distant, headquarters was Moscow.

The propagation of communism in the Asian lands faced, however, different problems from those which the communist party had known in Russia. The social and political background was different. The class structure was different. The industrial proletariat was very much smaller; the privileged and exploiting classes had to be classified in categories unfamiliar in Russia. It was uncertain what part each class would play in the revolution; it was uncertain even what classes existed. The early history of the Russian concern with Asia is of long polemical debates on the true reality of the affairs of these countries; in this time the role of communism was to be as much that of tutor to the Asian intelligentsia as that of conspirator and executive. It was to guide the Asian mind in making clear the nature of the revolution and the path which revolutionaries should follow.

The great issue was what to do with countries where all the would-be revolutionaries came from the bourgeoisie and where decades of work were necessary before the masses, industrial or agrarian, threw up leaders. Nationalism, whether directed against an obsolete government or against a colonial power had almost a monopoly in attracting the bourgeoisie; it was the political force which mattered, and communism had to reckon with this as the great fact of the time. The nationalist parties looked several ways; some, out of reasons of self-interest, were anticommunist, some, perhaps out of a vagueness about what communism stood for, were well disposed to a communist solution. Out of this situation, and of the constant disputes in Moscow, there emerged the idea of a discriminating, but only a transient, alliance between some of the bourgeois parties and communism, which would overthrow the backward governments of the time, classed variously as feudal, bureaucratic or colonial. Later it was taken for granted that there would be a rift between the bourgeois parties and the communists, and that the communists would become supreme. How this was to happen—the timing of the alliance, the timing of its rupture, the identification of the bourgeois parties to be selected as the catspaws of the communists—was the main subject of very lively debates of the period, on which reputations in the international communist movement depended, and which made or marred the fortunes of many would-be leaders of revolution. It may be said that the clear recognition of nationalism as a force to be reckoned with, the recognition that it was a force which was permanent and not undesirable—a view alien to leninism, however much this was hedged at times for reasons of expediency—was the distinctive feature of the great adventure of communism in seeking new land to conquer.

The issue was complicated by imperialism. Asia had to be delivered from the imperialists. Imperialism dominated its life; and the clash between nationalism and imperialism was the great issue of the time, out of which communism might seek to emerge. But the existence of imperialism in an entrenched position, the fact that most of the lands were under some kind of foreign domination, conditioned the whole of politics. Communism had to come to terms with them, and the history of the day is not clear without taking account of communism and the national question, communism and the ending of imperialism, communism and its attitude towards liberators from the foreign enemy who did not chance also to be communists themselves.

Communism might have made greater progress if the Soviet government had at first taken a less intransigent line towards Islam. But its doctrinaire atheism prevailed, and stirred up resistance in all muslim countries. Russia's handling of Islam was not to become flexible until after the second world war.

Though the Russian direction was exercised partly in secrecy, its mode of operation was clear. The guiding centre was the Communist International, the famous Comintern. This had its Far Eastern Bureau in Shanghai. From time to time during the years which followed the Russian revolution there were partial revelations of the Soviet network throughout Asia. Some of these came in the course of a famous trial in Kuomintang China—the Noulens case—others from the

trial of a remarkable Soviet spy in Japan, Richard Sorge.*
There were glimpses of couriers, codes, agents coming and
going from the Comintern. Another active international
organisation, at least in the early days of communism, was
the League for the Liberation of the East, which Stalin had
caused to be founded in 1917. This, after a period of dor-
mancy, was revived in 1927 as the League against Imperialism, which though fierce in manifesto proved rather
ineffective in action. There was the Pan-Pacific Trade Union
Secretariat, with headquarters in Shanghai, and there was
the South Seas Communist Group, with headquarters in
Singapore. Institutions in Russia—nominally academic—
trained very large numbers of young intellectuals from the
Asian countries who would return to their own countries as
agitators and organisers. The chief of these were the Lenin
University and the Sun Yat-sen University (whose first
rector was Radek and which was attended by thousands of
Chinese annually). This latter was the successor of the
University for the Toilers of the East in Moscow, which was
founded by the celebrated Indian revolutionary, M. N. Roy,
and specialised in educating students from Soviet central
Asia and south-east Asia. Over and above these was the
Academy of Red Professors, whose graduates constituted
the elite of the Comintern and provided the teaching staff
for the other party institutions. The course of study at the
Academy lasted nine years.

Ramifying and elaborate though this network may have
been, the main system by which Moscow exercised control
was, in its principal elements, much simpler. The Comintern

---

* Richard Sorge was a German who, posing as a nazi, imposed himself on the confidence of the German ambassador in Tokyo before
and during the war. He is said to have informed Russia that Japan
did not intend to attack it in 1941, and that may have contributed
to Russia's decision not to move troops from the German front.
Sorge was detected more or less by accident. He died in captivity of
alcoholism and heart disease.

press laid down the general lines of party policy, and local communist parties throughout Asia were left to implement it. The greater part of Moscow's work was done, not by agents working according to a plan, but by ideas which spread by their own force.

Events had in fact shaped as some of the strategists of communist revolution had hoped. The revolution in Russia had brought communism to life as an indigenous movement in Asia, especially in China—small at first but increasing as the years went by. Its impact has been described by Sardar K. M. Panikkar:

> The Russian Revolution quickened the pulse of the peoples of Asia. It awakened the masses, and created doubts in the minds of thinking people about the validity of many things which they had accepted without question from the West. It weakened the hold of the West upon the peoples of Asia.[1]

The revolution began to be regarded as one of the great liberating acts of history. It had caught the imagination of the Asian intelligentsia, even if at first imagination did not lead to action. Thereafter a part of the intellectuals looked towards Russia in a more kindly and hopeful way than towards the western countries, and was sceptical of some of the criticisms made of it until these were proved valid by rather more exercise of persuasion than should have been necessary. Political sympathy led to an interest in Russian culture. A writer like Dostoievsky appealed to Asian intellectuals, especially the Chinese; they sympathised with him and felt that he would have sympathised with them. Russian writers were less impressed by wealth than western ones, and believed that poor men and poor countries had a peculiar dignity. This was consoling. These feelings were reinforced by a new interest in Russia politically. After the revolution, Moscow gained credit in Asia by a number of gestures renouncing the gains by imperialist Russia in China, though when it came to negotiation the gestures meant less than had seemed.

Partly because of this climate, the Chinese Communist Party, the second communist party in non-Russian Asia (the first being the Indonesian), was founded in 1922. It came into being as the result of Chinese rather than Russian initiative, though Moscow sent two agents to take part in the initial organisation. They did their work so discreetly that they were not detected by the intelligence agencies of any of the foreign powers interested in China. At first the party consisted chiefly of Peking intellectuals. But they looked to Moscow for advice; by Moscow their leaders were made and unmade. This was to determine all the early history of communism in China.

2

The Chinese Communist Party:
First Phase

THE Chinese Communist Party in its first phase was very similar to other communist parties which sprang up in Asia during the 1920s.[1] Their leaders were not really men of action, at least on the grand scale. The first Asians to be fascinated by marxist doctrine were intellectuals, mostly at the universities, either as professors or students. The party was a haphazard collection of genuine marxists and every variety of revolutionary—anarchists, syndicalists, humanitarian idealists. To secure unity of action, it became increasingly necessary to insist on adherence to dogma. Those who would not subscribe were weeded out. This caused the early history of the party to be one of bitter intellectual dispute rather than of effective revolutionary action.

At this stage some of the members believed that disputation was the essential business of a communist party. Their approach was intellectual. They wanted to be precise about the new communist doctrine, to dissect and grasp it. Though they may not have understood their own mental processes, most of them seem to have had an underlying supposition that the thorough grasping of the ideas was enough in itself. They were both impressed and misled by the fact that in Russia the ideas of communism had overthrown the tsarist empire; they assumed in a vague way that, if correct communist ideas were disseminated, the ideas would have a life of their own, and that the walls of capitalism and imperialism would fall without the Asian communists' having done much more than propagate the doctrine. They confused the struggle for intellectual illumination with the struggle for political power. They were unaware that the essence of communism, as understood by Lenin, is the gaining of power by whatever means offer themselves at a particular moment. Even if they were willing to take to active conspiracy, they were obsessed with the idea that power must be sought by orthodox means which had to be found out from the marxist scriptures. That true communist conspiracy is an obsession with power, a lightning understanding of how to get it at a given moment, and a willingness to twist all theory to justify the action which a cool consideration of events dictated, was quite beyond their understanding.

There was another reason too for the obliquity of the early Chinese leaders. Sensitive about the backwardness of their countries, they resented the idea that tactics other than those suitable in Europe might be suitable in Asia. What was good for Europe must be good for them too; otherwise it might be thought that Asia was inferior. Hence, for many years there was a striking poverty of thinking among the communist intellectuals in China about the problems of their own continent. They were inhibited from striking out with ideas of their own in case they should seem to be accepting the principle that they belonged to second-class countries which needed a second-class communism.

The Chinese Communist Party therefore turned to Moscow for advice; and the advice received was the worst which could have been given. Moscow at that time was inclined to assume that all communist revolutions, in whatever country and whatever circumstances, must follow the pattern of Lenin and the bolsheviks at Petrograd in 1917.

What was this pattern of revolution? A communist revolution, said the leninists, could be made only by a conspiratorial party. That was the essence. The starting point was the existence of a communist party, organised with more than military discipline. Its members were to be professionals, not amateurs, and were to devote their lives exclusively to the party. Revolution meant plotting. It meant secrecy. It meant underground work. It meant the sudden coup d'état rather than the protracted battles of a major civil war. It did not matter if the communist party was small. It could hope, through excellence in organisation and plotting, to seize power by insurrection at a moment of crisis when the existing government had suffered some shattering blow to its prestige. Mass backing was not essential. All that was needed was to marshal the necessary force at the correct moment to seize the key positions, which circumstances might cause at that moment to be weakly defended. Strikes in public utilities and key industries to paralyse suddenly the life of the community, the storming of ministries by action squads of workers—that might be enough.

In other words, the revolution was not to be a mass uprising of the people, but was to be planned and initiated by a small minority. Of course, this minority would not by itself have the physical force to complete the revolution. But according to the leninist doctrine it should use as its instrument the mass organisations of the workers. Here a vital distinction was made, which was to affect communist history deeply. It was assumed that by 'workers' was meant the urban workers, not the peasants. The exclusion of the peasants as a revolutionary class was a peculiar feature of Russian revolutionary practice. The leninists took it for granted that during the dynamic period of revolution and subsequent change and reform, the peasants would at best acquiesce in what was done. Though revolution might be made in their name and allegedly for their benefit, and though the government might be called one of 'workers and peasants', the peasants were not a revolutionary class. Their way of living made them backward and non-creative. They were objects of history, not its makers.

The most succinct expression of this view is by Lenin himself. 'The city', he says, 'inevitably leads the village. The village inevitably follows the city. The only question is, which of the urban classes will the village follow.' In fairness to Lenin, it must be said that the emphasis of his views sometimes changed. In the *Theses on the National and Colonial Questions*, written in 1920, he said that in backward countries a Soviet government could establish itself if it obtained peasant support. But it was evidently the urban communists who were to lead, and the peasants to support.

These concepts of how to make a revolution bear very heavily the stamp of the society in which they had germinated. The theory, and the structure and modes of action of the Soviet Communist Party, had been determined by the peculiar conditions of pre-communist Russia. In Russia under the tsars, a party with the aims of the bolshevists could not exist except as a conspiracy. Constitutional action was out of the question; a duma in which communists obtained a majority would have been promptly abolished.

This was the pattern which Moscow tried to wish upon the Chinese communists, and at first they accepted it. They wanted an almost blind imitation of the October revolution in Russia. The aim was conspiracy and the coup d'état, not a broad-based popular movement. Perhaps that was natural. The bolshevik revolution had the prestige of success. It was thought that it had shown that plots could succeed, if made at the right moment, while great popular movements usually failed because governments could suppress them more easily. Yet even at the time it might have been questioned both in Moscow and China whether a revolution which had succeeded in one set of circumstances would automatically succeed in others. The bolshevik revolution was carried through in a society which for some years had had a form of parliamentary life. It took place in a society where there was already industry, a centralised system of government and reasonably good communications. In China the circumstances were in no way parallel.

The Chinese leaders accepted the blind instruction of Moscow and allowed themselves to be propelled towards disaster. They scarcely questioned the Russian advice. It took a surprising time for doubts to grow up or to affect their confidence. And until these doubts accumulated and strategy was modified, communism did not prosper.

During this period, communist energies were spent chiefly in organising communist trade unions in coastal towns on the periphery of vast hinterlands, such as in Canton or Shanghai. Because of the part which the Petrograd workers had played in Lenin's revolution, there was an obsession with the urban proletariat, still a minute class relative to the whole population. Revolts were brought about in cities, as in Canton in 1927. It was quite futile. Those observers who presciently saw that communism in China really was a danger were often written down as fanatics and scaremongers. Revolts such as the communists then organised could not have led to nation-wide revolution, for, even if they had succeeded initially, the government could collect overwhelming force from the hinterland to crush rebellious ports or industrial cities or barracks or dockyards.

Where the Russian theorists showed themselves blind was in not perceiving that the same fate would have befallen the bolshevik insurrection in Russia in 1917 if it had not been for the fact that Russia had lost a war and that the tsarist army had collapsed. This fact, and this fact alone, had made the Russian revolution possible. The Comintern strategists refused to perceive this.

The change in the fortunes of the communists in China came about when the Chinese began to strike out for themselves. This came about partly as a result of the turbulent history of China in these years, and partly because of the pressures brought to bear by the government for exterminating communism. Under this threat the communist party had either to perish or to free itself from too much theory. It had to transfer the leadership to men with a natural genius for political action, unencumbered by philosopy even while using its phrases.

This metamorphosis of the Chinese Communist Party happened as a result of its involvement in the great central revolutionary drama of the 1920s in China. In this drama, communism did not hold the centre of the stage. The communists were still at the time a secondary revolutionary party. The true revolutionary party in the 'twenties was the Nationalist Party, the Kuomintang. Its historical role has to be understood in the light of the history of the times, and in the reason for, and fierceness of, Chinese nationalism.

China after the fall of the Manchu emperors in 1911 had lapsed into anarchy. Power was fragmented. Local generals and local governors made themselves autonomous. In China's helpless condition, its rights were grossly injured by the outside powers, especially by Japan. The people of China, proud in spite of their apparent irresponsibility, remembered the insults and were determined to find means of avenging them.

The appeal of the Kuomintang was therefore in the first place national. Its mandate was to put China on a footing of equality with the great powers. By its success in this it was to be judged. As this aim was shared by people of all classes, so did the backing for the Kuomintang cut across classes. It was the national party, founded by the incarnation of the national spirit, Sun Yat-sen, and anybody who felt himself a nationalist could join it. It included millionaires, bankers, professors, teachers, peasants. Just because of this heterogeneous character, it could have no detailed social policy, except to preserve things as they were because to change them might have risked disrupting the alliance. And that was the Kuomintang's great weakness: it could not attach to itself the fervour of any of the classes which felt an intolerable sense of grievance because to do so would for certain have alienated others. True, the Kuomintang spoke officially of social doctrines, but it was all in the air and hardly meant for practical application. Anybody who wishes to satisfy himself of this should read Sun Yat-sen's *San Min Chi I*—the official scripture of the Kuomintang.

In organisation—but not in ideology—the Kuomintang had been remodelled in the early 1920s deliberately upon the lines of the Communist Party of the Soviet Union. Sun Yat-sen had been impressed by the effectiveness of the Russian party as a revolutionary instrument; he saw in it the kind of organisation required for the regeneration and government of an Asian country in confusion. His perception of this, and his action upon his perception, give him his claim to greatness in the Asian history of our times. In return for making use of Russia in this way, he was ready for intimate co-operation with the Russian government, and he was convinced that this would be possible without the Kuomintang's being subverted by communism. 'The experienced leaders of the Soviet Union are interested in working with our party', he said, 'not with the inexperienced students of the Chinese Communist Party.'

Because the Kuomintang claimed to be quite simply the party of nationalism, it was easy for communists to join it; they too claimed to be nationalists. Under the camouflage of their nationalism—which was more than camouflage because it was genuine—the communists, though still a fairly small group, hoped to permeate the Kuomintang, to obtain some of the key posts in the party, and at the right moment to seize control of the party, and purge it of its rightists. They planned to use its great impetus to carry themselves up. The Kuomintang was the rocket; the communists saw themselves as the warhead which it carried.

That was their justification for the alliance between communism and the bourgeois classes in the Kuomintang. It was invented, approved and directed by the celebrated Russian agent, Michael Borodin. It was an innovation because it introduced a quite new set of ideas in communist ideology. It is true that the germ of these ideas is to be found in Lenin. Lenin was more a revolutionary journalist than a systematic theorist, and in his voluminous writings there can be found a warrant for most actions by communist parties in all possible circumstances. Lenin had been interested in China as a key country for the overthrow of imperialism, with which capitalism was linked. He said that as the twentieth century wore on there would be a succession of 'national liberation wars' waged against colonial and semi-colonial governments. The communists, he said, must take part in these wars, in any country where they happened, and must ally themselves with the nationalist forces, even if these were chiefly of the middle class and anticommunist. The communists, he said, should make use of these wars in order to 'educate' and organise the peasantry and the broad masses of exploited peoples in a revolutionary spirit.

Nevertheless, Lenin did not systematise these ideas or explore them very deeply, and the Bolshevik Party in Russia had gained power by its own exertions. It was in Asia that there was to develop from this time onwards a preoccupation with the exact manner of the relation between communism and national parties, and the way in which communism might exploit 'nationalism'. This concern has continued ever since.

The correctness of communist strategy in China in these years—between 1924 and 1926—became a matter of deep concern in Moscow. This was the time when the prospects of communism in Asia most interested the Russian government. It was not so much that Russia was increasingly interested in Asia, but that Stalin and Trotsky were engaged in a life and death struggle. Since China was the question of the hour, each of them took opposite sides in the controversy, hoping to use it to discredit his opponent. 'If Stalin said this', said one observer of the conflict, 'Trotsky said that.'[2]

Stalin, who approved the line followed, argued that in a backward and pre-capitalist country the stages of revolution could not be skipped. China must pass through a bourgeois phase before it could become communist. According to orthodox communist theory, the Kuomintang represented the middle class and was carrying out a typical struggle of the middle class against a 'feudal' governing class. Actually, the analysis was wrong-headed: the warlords were the extraordinary product of anarchy; they were not feudal. But Stalin accepted the view that communism should work with the Kuomintang in order to carry through a bourgeois revolution as a prelude to the proletarian one which would follow. By collaborating with the Kuomintang, it would force the pace of the revolution, and in the end bring about communism all the more quickly. But if, on the other hand, the communists sided with the forces of subversion against the Kuomintang, they would merely be suppressed because the situation was not yet ripe for revolution.

Trotsky, on the contrary, argued for immediate proletarian revolution.* According to him, the bourgeois phase

* Stalin's attitude was, however, ambivalent. He laid more stress on peasant movements than other Russian leaders of the time. He spoke of a 'revolution of the masses of farmers and workers numbering many millions'. He said that communist victory was impossible without an agrarian movement. But he argued also that revolutionary peasant committees were insufficient to 'permeate the ocean of peasantry'. The peasants must be led by a party whose basis was the urban proletariat. Certainly it was hard for one who, like Stalin, was the hammer of the peasants to sound entirely sincere when he spoke of the peasants as a revolutionary force.

could be cut out altogether. The proletariat, if properly led, could seize power at one spring. It was unnecessary to collaborate with the Kuomintang.

Stalin's view comes out very clearly in an account of a meeting of the Chinese Subcommittee of the Comintern, held about this time in Moscow. It is summarised as follows by Robert North in his book *Moscow and Chinese Communists*. The problem discussed was the Comintern's attitude to direct revolutionary action by the Chinese peasants.

> At the meeting, Bukharin informed his two colleagues, Togliatti of Italy and Treint of France, that the peasants of China were forcibly seizing the land. 'If we do not curb the agrarian movement', he said, 'we will lose our allies of the left wing of the Kuomintang, and it will be impossible for us to win a majority in the Kuomintang. On the other hand, by curbing it we will enlarge our influence in it.'
>
> As the discussion proceeded, Bukharin insisted that the Subcommittee ought to hear Stalin's opinion. When he joined them he supported the arguments put forward by Bukharin. 'To fail to take a position against the peasant revolt', he said, 'would be to set the left bourgeoisie against us. That would mean civil war. The armed Chinese are largely mercenaries, and we do not dispose of big enough financial resources to buy them for our side.'
>
> 'But the mercenaries', Treint pointed out, 'are largely ruined peasants who will desert to the communists if the agrarian program is put forward.'
>
> Stalin argued that the left bourgeoisie were still too powerful. 'Its armies will not disband in the twinkle of an eye, and we will then be defeated in a civil war before the insurgent agrarians are able to connect with the proletarian insurrection.'

'The communists can manoeuvre, however', said Stalin, 'without compromising anything. The agrarian revolution frightens the Kuomintang only to the degree that it directly injures its members as well as the officers of the army. I propose to send instructions to Borodin to oppose the confiscation and division of land belonging to members of the Kuomintang or the officers of the Nationalist army. We possess sufficient authority over the Chinese masses to make them accept our decision.'[3]

On Stalin's side there was also a more subtle argument for working with the Kuomintang. Stalin is still a curiously misunderstood figure. He was often pretentious and absurd as a theorist, but he was shrewd in grasping some basic facts. Watching the Kuomintang army, which at that time looked like a revolutionary army partly because it was impelled forward by its communist allies, Stalin became increasingly interested in the idea that an army—a native army and not an intervening Russian one—might be the agent by which revolution could be carried out. Hitherto it had been taken for granted that an army would be under the control of the government which was to be subverted; the revolution must be made by civilians struggling as an underground band of conspirators against an armed government. But it dawned on Stalin that China had shown that these circumstances were not universal. In China there had come into being an army which was on the side of the revolution. The army was, in fact, the 'armed revolution'. Stalin described this in a passage which has become famous.

> In China the struggle is not being carried on by un-armed people against the troops of their own government, but the armed people in the form of its revolutionary army is in action. In China, armed revolution is fighting against armed counter-revolution. The Chinese revolutionists, including the communists, must make a special study of things military. They must not

regard military questions as something of secondary importance, for military questions in China are at present the most important factor in the Chinese revolution.

Stalin's hopes in 1926 miscarried. The army, which he hoped might carry out the communist revolution, passed out of the clutches of the communists. But for a time it was touch and go.

The communists had wormed their way into the Kuomintang; they advanced by leaps and bounds from being an obscure group into a nation-wide organisation. When Kuomintang groups went to agitate in the villages to undermine the position of the warlords whom they were overthrowing, communist agents accompanied them to stir up the demand for land reform and the overthrow of the landlord classes. Their young intellectuals, as political commissars with the army, began to make the army political. At headquarters, they began to gain high positions. Chou En-lai became the political head at the officers' training academy at Whampoa, whose commandant was Chiang Kai-shek; the cream of the new army passed through it, and Chou En-lai's personal relations with many of the officers, including Chiang Kai-shek himself, was to be in the next years one of the secret but very important strands in China's tangled history.

In 1926 the Kuomintang, striking out from Canton, made its northern expedition, which conquered all south China and the Yangtze valley, and enabled the new government which it set up to claim international recognition. In 1927, just before the Kuomintang occupied Shanghai, which lay at its mercy, its leaders decided that the time had arrived for a break with the communists. They had not been as much deceived about the communist intentions as the communists had supposed; they had been made vigilant by the excesses of the Peasant Unions which the communists had

organised; small landowners were the core of the Kuomintang, and any movement against landlords made them
apprehensive. They had gathered even more sinister news
about communist conspiracy. One story is that a high official
of the Comintern, the Indian M. N. Roy, received a telegram
of instructions from Stalin, and carelessly revealed it to a
leftist but non-communist leader of the Kuomintang, Wang
Ching-wei, whom he wrongly believed to be a sympathiser
with the communists. Wang Ching-wei informed Chiang
Kai-shek. Chiang preferred an alliance with the Shanghai
bankers and the hope of an understanding with the western
powers to the dangerous alliance with the communists. He
struck quickly, expelled the communists from the party,
and organised a terror against them.

Chiang Kai-shek's surprise attack proved deadly. Some
of the future eminent figures of the Chinese communist
government escaped almost by a miracle. Chou En-lai, for
example, was captured and condemned to be shot; by pure
chance, the officer who was to be responsible for his execu-
tion proved to be a former pupil of Chou's when he had been
teaching at the Whampoa Military Academy, and he
allowed Chou to escape. Many leading cadres were not so
fortunate. The whole plan on which the communists had
until then been working fell in ruins. Characteristically,
Stalin, from Moscow, blamed the disaster on the clumsiness
of the Chinese communists.

But the communist snake was scotched, not killed. The
communists saved something from the wreckage—enough
to be the nucleus of the Chinese People's Republic which
eventually was to be proclaimed in Peking. Enough of the
leaders escaped from the terror and persevered with politics.
Units of the Kuomintang army in Hunan and the Yangtze
valley mutinied and declared for the communists. They
retired to the mountains, and were joined by a growing
number of landless and desperate peasants. They were able
to take possession of the inaccessible border land of the

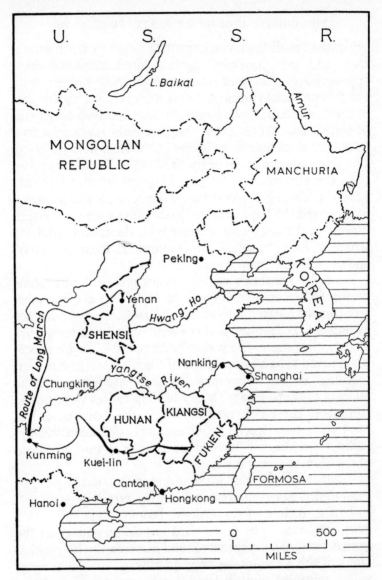

CHINA: DISPOSITION OF COMMUNIST-DOMINATED AREAS
BETWEEN THE BREAK WITH THE KUOMINTANG IN 1926 AND
THE JAPANESE INVASION OF 1937, SHOWING THE ROUTE OF
THE LONG MARCH

provinces of Kiangsi and Fukien, and they set up there the first Chinese soviet government. Border territory—where surveillance by the central authorities is weakest—has played a vital part in communist strategy.

An historical eye might have seen in this the beginnings of a force such as has on several occasions in previous Chinese history brought about the fall of a regime. In Kiangsi this force was to work out the political and military strategy which, after twenty years, many vicissitudes and the great epic of the Long March from the Yangtze to the remote north-west of China, was to make communism the master of the country.

3

The Chinese Communist Party:
Second Phase

THE man responsible for giving communism in China its new course was Mao Tse-tung, though when the split with the Kuomintang happened it was still to be some time before he became head of the Chinese Communist Party. By discovering the revolutionary tactics which would succeed in China, and by persuading his colleagues to accept them, Mao won his place in history.

And what a place it is! He may claim to have given a new slant to the affairs of Asia, and the effects of his life are likely to be felt enduringly.

The history of communism in Asia is larger than that of the men taking part in it; they have served it as pawns, and have been anonymous in the process. Mao Tse-tung is the exception, and our story of communism in China must take in a short biographical sketch of him. He is a rich and varied figure, and no very satisfactory life has yet appeared. The material for his life and ideas is not scanty, but the reader is apt to be overwhelmed by the various impressions of him. He has a mind which responds instinctively to realities. He is a man of action who uses ideas for his own purpose, not a man of ideas who has turned to action as the apostle of his theories, as was the case with most of his predecessors in the leadership of the Chinese Communist Party; and in this he resembles Lenin. His basic ideas are relatively simple. But to make simple ideas prevail as a guide to action has often been a justified claim to greatness.

Mao was born in 1893, a native of Hunan, which throughout the nineteenth century was celebrated for producing the most vigorous men of action of the day, including some eminent revolutionaries. At many periods of his life he was to be conscious of the destiny which geography thus seemed to impose upon him. He was a peasant's son. His father had served for a year in the army, and as a result had brought back with him enough capital to acquire a farm of three-and-a-half acres. In Chinese rural society this established him as well-to-do; the soil of Hunan is extremely productive, and he made a good deal of money in trading in rice and pigs. This fairly prosperous origin has proved rather an embarrassment to Mao, and it is played down in communist writings.

His father's avarice was an irritant to Mao Tse-tung in his early years. Because of it he developed by reaction a consistent indifference to material property. He also rebelled against his father's conformism, and at first, when he became interested in politics, had an inclination towards anarchism. But he was himself sufficiently a conformist to want to accept a political outlook as a complete whole, and was not content with an eclectic method of building from here and there. Thus, he says that he ran through six systems of thought before finally he came down to marxism. They were buddhism, monarchism, republicanism, pacifist idealism, democracy and anarchism. His strength lay in insisting, more or less by instinct, on educating himself not from books but from practical experience.

29

Throughout the nineteenth century and still today, Hunan has been intellectually the most active and free-thinking of China's provinces. Mao picked up a fairly good education at its capital, Chang-Sha. A young man so receptive to ideas cannot have failed to make his mark upon his contemporaries, but they have left singularly little information about him. But one record is interesting: a friend of his called Siao-Yu describes how the two of them went on a walking tour of Hunan province which was designed to acquaint them with the condition of the peasants. One evening they were stopping at a country inn, and it came out that a young daughter of the innkeeper had a reputation for telling fortunes by reading people's faces. With a little reluctance she was persuaded to prophesy Mao Tse-tung's fate: 'Your physiognomy', she said, 'indicates that you can become a great officer, a prime minister, or a great bandit chief. You are very audacious, and have great ambition, but you have no sentiment at all. You could kill ten thousand or even a hundred thousand people without turning a single hair. But you are very patient. If you have not been killed by your enemies by the time you are thirty-five, you can consider yourself safe, and you will be lucky day by day. You will have at least six wives, but not many children. I see that you and your family do not get along well together. You will never live in your home town, and I see that you will have no fixed home.'[1] To Siao-Yu she gave an infinitely less dramatic fate. But nearly all the forecast of Mao has come true; his was to be a career sufficiently shaking for China and all Asia.

In spite of his adoption of marxism, Mao stuck to the empirical. He was always opposed to dogmatism. For him, ideas were only worthwhile if they could be used for action; otherwise he considered them bleak and unattractive. It is this which explains his subsequent career: he became a marxist, but he had always both feet on the ground, and was always willing to modify theory if it ran counter to

30

his strong political common-sense.* One pregnant remark sums up his outlook. 'There are people', he said, 'who think that marxism is a kind of magic truth with which we can cure any disease. We should tell them that doctors are more useless than cow dung. Dung can be used as fertiliser.'

Because of this, because of reservations which he made in his own mind, Mao was to break away, in fact if not in theory, from the Russian obsession—which is apparently the true deduction from Marx—that only the industrial proletariat can be the creative class in making a communist revolution. Mao accepted Marx as providing a general theory of revolution, and as telling the Chinese intelligentsia where they were and what they had to do. Marx had brought revolution into the lives of the Chinese intelligentsia, and had made them vividly conscious of the drama of the present age. No other prophet could compete with him in this; he gave the intellectual sanction to revolution. But in the Chinese countryside, revolt was nothing novel. Mao's inspiration, as Dr Kuo has pointed out, came as much from the stream of popular literature in China championing the peasant underdog as from Marx and Lenin. Marx was a townsman, a professional man, a philosopher; Mao's instincts were all the reverse of these. He saw no reason why the industrial proletariat had to be the hero of the Chinese revolution. He saw a different instrument to hand in the peasantry, and he deliberately turned away from the towns to the country.

Whether he realised the evasion and the leap which he was making is not clear. He would not abandon Marx, for Marx had come to him in his youth as the source of revolu-

* One of the best assessments of Mao is given by Dr P. C. Kuo in his excellent book, *China, New Age and New Outlook*: 'Mao's chief claim to greatness does not lie in his originality or in his capacity for minute analysis. It lies rather in the directness of his observation and thinking and the pertinence of his conclusions to the realities confronting him' (page 31; see Reading List).

tion. Probably he determined to improve on Marx and to write him afresh in peasant terms. But he was unable to avow this because communism does not permit compromise. Converting Marx to the use of the great class of Chinese peasantry had therefore to be done by subterfuge and without admitting what was being done. But conversion it was, none the less. That was Mao's great achievement, his life's work.

Mao always remained Chinese. He never deluded himself that they could act like a western people. He did not make the mistake, like some intellectuals, of thinking of Chinese society as a *tabula rasa*. He knew it from experience as something extremely tenacious, with characteristics not easily changed. His culture was that of popular, not Confucian, China. He had read repeatedly the great romantic novels, such as the saga translated under the title *All Men Are Brothers*. Quotations from them appeared in many of his speeches. They gave him the common terms for reference with the people to whom he appealed. From the adventure stories of these books he derived many ideas about political and military strategy, and applied them.

He had also a feeling, and even a semi-pious regard, for the classical tradition in China. He had repudiated it, but he understood it, and the understanding remained throughout his life; it gave him stature. The old-fashioned scholars of China understood him; they regarded him as pernicious, but they regarded him as understandable. It counted with them that as a young man he had visited the grave of Confucius and the birthplace of Mencius. A peculiarity of Mao was that he was no mean poet, celebrating the crises in life by writing poems, always using the classical forms. When he entered Peking as victor in 1949, a group of progressive poets greeted him with a poem in *avant garde* verse. He replied in almost too scrupulous classical Chinese. It was interpreted as a polite rebuke to extravagance.

This dual nature of Mao Tse-tung—nationalist and

revolutionary, child of China and champion of the most up-to-date form of social discipline imprinted in an alien continent—has been analysed with great acumen by Dr Stuart Schram, one of the forerunners of a lively French scholarship on China which will probably come into its own as a result of General de Gaulle's decision to recognise the Chinese revolution. Schram sums Mao up as follows:

Is he, as was Lenin, a revolutionary who merely uses nationalism for his own ends? Or is he above all a nationalist for whom Marxism-Leninism is merely a convenient slogan? Most certainly he is neither . . . he certainly does not see in nationalism merely a necessary evil, as did Lenin. The 'Glory of the Hans', to quote the title of the first chapter of this anthology, is clearly a living thing to him, a value no less precious than revolution . . . it could be argued that, if the categories in which he reasons are basically Marxist, his deepest emotional tie is still to the Chinese nation: and if he is bent on transforming China's society and economy in the shortest possible time in order to turn her into a powerful modern nation, he does so in order that she may once more resume her rightful place in the world.'

Here was a man who at once had the feeling for the realities of China and the knowledge of how to act success-fully in China, and at the same time the grasp of a twentieth-century doctrine which might revivify China. The special interest in studying his career is to watch the twin aspects of his character and to see how the one helped the other. In substance, Mao extended the communist revolution by turn-ing from the towns to the country. He saw that from the peasantry, heavily-laden with grievances which would in-cline them to communism, mass communist armies could be recruited. If they could be used properly, if they could be adequately armed, they could eventually seize the railways, the industrial towns, the ports, the administrative centres and the national capital. They could in the end overwhelm the government which at the start had seemed to possess overwhelming strength.

By these means Mao was to carry through his great revolution, and to be responsible for destruction and suffering on a scale comparable to that of the great monsters of Asia's past, such as Chinghiz Khan and Timur. Thus there came true the forecast of the innkeeper's daughter. Any statesman in Asia who sets his hand to communism must run the risk of finding himself a mass executioner. To do Mao justice, he realised this from the start. 'Revolution', he said in 1927, 'is not a dinner party, nor literary composition, nor painting, nor embroidery.' Mao made his revolution the rough way, the way of the peasants. It is silly to idealise it, for in India Gandhi has shown that revolution can be made with little bloodshed. Nevertheless, Mao's way must be studied.

It would be a mistake to suppose that the way was clear to him from the start. His ideas evolved slowly. They were invested in a certain haze which is pecular to all men of practical genius. Moreover, the communist party which Mao had to win to his way of thought was at first dominated by intellectuals for whom the charm of communism consisted precisely in its novelty and in its turning away from everything truly Chinese. Mao himself was probably attracted to, but not captivated by, marxism for this very reason. At the start he must have deviated uneasily, and was unwilling that his right leg should know the steps which his left leg was taking.

He first came to prominence in the Chinese Communist Party when, in the days of its collaboration with the Kuomintang, he was deputed to organise the peasantry of Hunan province for the revolution, and—ironically—to check the excesses being committed there by Peasant Unions.

This was his own province and, being a peasant, he did not need to make new studies of agrarian relations. This was the time when he changed his view about the role of the peasants in the insurrection. At first he had accepted the orthodox view and had believed that the urban classes must be the spearhead of revolution; for a time he had, like other early members of the party, concentrated upon forming urban trade unions. But practical experience sowed new ideas. His conversion was expressed in a document called *A Report on an Investigation of the Agrarian Movement in Hunan*, which was published in March 1927.

This is likely to remain one of the classics of communism in Asia, though it was repudiated at the time by the central committee of the Chinese Communist Party. The odd thing about it is that it hardly mentioned marxism. It might have been written by a man who had never heard of Marx. But it recognised, as a result of an analysis of the grievances of the peasantry and of their capacity for action, the enormous havoc which an enraged peasantry might make, and the political power which could be generated if peasant vitality could be harnessed.

> The force of the peasantry is like that of the raging winds and driving rain. It is rapidly increasing in violence. No force can stand in its way. The peasantry will tear apart all nets which bind it and hasten along the road to liberalism. They will bury beneath them all forces of imperialism, militarism, corrupt officialdom, village bosses and evil gentry. Every revolutionary party, every revolutionary comrade will be subjected to their scrutiny and be accepted or rejected by them. Shall we stand in the vanguard and lead them or stand behind them and oppose them? Every Chinese is free to pick his answer. However, destiny will force us to pick an answer soon . . . The broad masses of the peasantry have arisen to fulfil their historic destiny.[3]

Mao went so far as to say that in carrying out a revolution in China, the contribution of the urban dwellers and of an organised revolutionary army could at best be only one third of the effective effort: the other two thirds would come from the peasantry. He never disguised how brutal the revolution would be. 'It cannot be done delicately', he said, 'or gently, kindly, politely, plainly and modestly.' 'If the peasants do not acquire great force', he said at the same time, 'the power of the landlords, consolidated over thousands of years, can never be uprooted. There must be a tidal wave over the countryside.'

Here was a strategy of revolution different from that of Lenin, even though Lenin had spoken, with varying force, about the usefulness of the peasantry as an instrument for revolutionaries. Mao's view had indeed become more like that of the romantic pre-leninists: there would be a mass uprising, not a narrow but effective conspiracy. Mao pointed out that the communist party should and could lead the insurrection, but he seems to have thought that a rising would happen whether or not it was stirred up by a political party. The role of the communist party was to see that the inevitable peasant uprising was used to create a communist state. It would ensure that the peasants, once they had secured a redress of their grievances against landlords and moneylenders, did not settle down into a comfortable conservatism, as is usually the instinct of peasants everywhere.

In the years after 1927 Mao developed out of these basic views a new guide to revolution. The new strategy, he said, must be 'to encircle the cities from the countryside'.

To this broad conception, Mao added a number of conditions which had to be fulfilled if the concept was to be translated into action. One of these was that peasant discontent must be linked with a systematic doctrine, such as that of communism. Otherwise it would result in a momentary outbreak which would lead to nothing; it would be a passing expression of despair. The peasant revolts of the nineteenth century were a good example. The largest of them, the Taiping rebellion, gropingly felt the need of a doctrine, and attached itself to a grotesque form of christianity, adapted from the teachings of western missionaries. But this christianity did not have enough political content to give it creative power.

> Most guerilla wars in ancient times ended in failure [wrote Mao]. Only in the big countries of modern times where communist parties have emerged, like the Soviet Union during its civil war and China at present, can guerilla wars achieve victories. There have been in history many peasant wars of the roving insurgent type, but they all failed. In the present age of advanced communications and technology, it is more than ever an entirely groundless illusion to attempt to win victory after the fashion of the roving insurgents.[4]

A second condition was that the peasant armies, once formed, must operate from a base. They must carve out their own home area from which to recruit their force and launch their campaigns. This base must be secure. That was of great importance. It is true that this was not an entirely original conception of Mao. The Comintern, reviewing the disaster of the Chinese Communist Party in 1927, had laid down—by hind-sight—a rather similar principle. But it was Mao who acted upon it.

The first attempts by Mao to organise revolution in the early 'thirties failed because his base—in Kiangsi province in the Yangtze valley—was very insecure. In this first Chinese soviet state, the Chinese communists tried out many of their policies, and the knowledge they gained from experience was to help them later. But the party was too much harried by attack from outside to be able to concentrate on domestic plans. A better base had to be found. From Kiangsi the communists migrated, by the famous

Long March of 1935, to the much more remote area of northern Shensi, where their flanks were protected by Outer Mongolia, under Soviet control, and where they could receive supplies from the USSR. Thus the base was made secure, and a long step was taken towards the revolution's triumph, though this was realised by few at the time.*

The Long March had a profound influence on the Chinese imagination. It made the communists the heroes of China; even while they continued to be reprobated by public opinion, they nonetheless forced themselves into the fore-front of national awareness. They became part of the folk-lore of modern China. The Long March was such a stupen-dous achievement that it reduced to almost laughable in-significance the efforts of other Chinese political groups. Scenes from it dominated the Chinese mind in much the same way as events in the Spanish Civil War haunted the imagination of men and women in Europe in the 'thirties.

A third condition for Mao Tse-tung's type of revolu-tion was that a country should be large and should have poor communications. Mao stressed this in all his writings. He admitted that in a small country, or in a country where communications were such that a government could quickly mobilise great force in any given area, his particular strategy would be out of place. (This was to be proved true later during the communist rebellion in Malaya.) His type of revolutionary action needed much elbow room and China was ideal for the purpose.

These were not the limits of the innovations by Mao. In writings during the Sino-Japanese war, he invented a new theory, that of the 'New Democracy'. Revolution, he said, should be brought about, not by one class only, but by a union of several revolutionary classes. Those which he identified as eligible to join this revolutionary coalition

* In the later period, after 1945, the base was shifted from Shensi to Manchuria. This was even more secure because of its proximity to Russia. How far Russia was consulted is controversial.

were the town workers, the peasants, the petty bourgeoisie and the so-called patriotic bourgeoisie. The classes against which they were to act were landlords, bureaucratic capitalists and Kuomintang leaders.[5]

This theory is not at all orthodox. Nothing like it is to be found in Marx. Admittedly, the theory was to remain little more than a theory; though Mao Tse-tung, after his victory, tried to give expression to it by admitting some radical but non-communist parties to the Chinese government, they have been there chiefly for show and have had no real share of power. When they became critical of the communist leadership, they were very quickly disciplined. The theory, like Mao's other innovations, was put forward for tactical and opportunistic reasons; it was a way of rallying the maximum support against the Kuomintang. Nevertheless, the remarkable freedom of Mao in reformulating communist dogma for his own convenience showed a capacity in the communist movement in China to free itself from the rigidity of theories. A bold leader could take what advantage he could gain from them—and then act according to his own judgment of expediency.*

Mao followed his principles remorselessly and ruthlessly. He transformed the nature of the revolution. For a time after 1927, the central committee of the Chinese Communist Party had remained in Shanghai. But Mao had retreated to the hills in the interior. The central committee produced nothing but resolutions. Mao produced action. The central committee was not a threat to the Kuomintang. Mao

* Mao gave an interesting theoretical justification of his new doctrine. He argued, like an orthodox marxist, that the revolution in China must be in two stages: feudalism must be overthrown by capitalism, and capitalism must be overthrown by socialism. But he said that in China the two revolutions could go on simultaneously. The corollary was that the form of government proper to China should be a coalition of the communist party with other patriotic and democratic parties which might co-operate in one or other revolution.

harried the Kuomintang. By 1932, the real centre of communist power in China had become clear to all, and the central committee removed from Shanghai and joined Mao in the Kiangsi soviet. That was the turning point in his career; but he had to wait until the middle of The Long March to achieve recognised ascendancy.

Mao turned the smouldering discontent in rural China into a storm of terror. Wherever the communists went, at least in the early years, they let loose a *jacquerie* in the countryside. Executions were on the grand scale. Communism appealed to the savage desire of the exploited Chinese to kill their oppressors. The enormities won the communists many fanatical recruits. But the terror also frightened off many of the intellectuals and urban middle class who might otherwise have supported communism. Therefore, after the Long March the communists modified their policy. Only the rich or pro-Japanese landlords and money-lenders were harried. The others were reassured—and preserved to be caught and ruined in the land reform and proscription which took place when the communists had finally seized power at the centre.

An innovator like Mao Tse-tung who openly admits that his theories are in part innovation and who does not try to smuggle them in as being really orthodox, was bound, in a rigid system like communism, to meet with resistance and hostility. At times Mao had to fight the rival factions in his own party with the same resolution as he used against Chiang Kai-shek, and he seems to have been no less ruthless. But his theories prevailed in guiding the actions of the Chinese Communist Party, even though more orthodox theorists continued to be tolerated and even acclaimed.

The great ideological struggle took place in the 'thirties. But many years later there was a curious echo or revelation of it. At the Eighth Congress of the Chinese Communist Party, held in Peking in the late summer of 1956, the assembly was presented with an unexpected speaker, a ghost from the past—Li Li-san, a leader in the early days of the party, a specialist in organising trade unions and in urban agitation, who had personified the views which Mao had set himself to combat. Li made a confession of his former errors. He said that he had been carried away by 'subjectivism'. Unlike Mao, he had not been a careful student of realities.

Such fanatic subjectivism expressed itself politically in treating wishful thinking as the real world, and making decisions and taking action without regard to consequences. It all came from fleeting moments of fanaticism. Such a blind, impetuous and degenerate way of doing things ignored the actual situation and conditions facing us. In cities where the white terror was strongly entrenched, instead of taking pains to carry on hard work among the masses, and to build up the revolutionary forces bit by bit, the opposite was done: strikes and demonstrations were called and uprisings repeatedly organised. In the rural areas, instead of going all out to set the peasant masses in motion to urge a revolutionary struggle for land reform, to develop guerilla warfare and gradually build up revolutionary bases, the revolutionary armed forces, young and numerically small at that time, were ordered to storm the major cities without end. Then, instead of turning back after having been repeatedly and badly battered and knocked about, desperate and headlong attempts were made to carry on the struggle to the end. As a result, the revolutionary forces suffered serious losses.

In organisational matters, such fantastic subjectivism took the form of strong sectarianism. I could hardly keep a cool head and listen to the opinions of others. When comrades put forward different views, they

would be accused at random of opportunism and mis-
guided compromise. They would be discriminated
against and vilified. And so an extremely abnormal
situation arose in the Party and even caused a number
of excellent cadres to meet their death.[6]

In the speech, Li Li-san put down his subjectivism and
the mistakes which he had committed to his unsound origin.
He came from the petty bourgeoisie: its 'foul traits' of class-
consciousness, conceit and self-complacency were like wild
grass 'that even after a prairie fire revives at the first breath
of spring'. But this was Li Li-san's rather poetical way of
conceding that he had been permanently defeated by Mao
Tse-tung.

These were the ideas and strategy—with which the Chinese
Communist Party fought its great fight for supremacy. It
lasted a long while—more than twenty years from the time
of the breach with the Kuomintang. For most of this time,
the chances of a communist victory seldom appeared bright.
Russia regarded the Kuomintang as the regime with which
it would have to deal for a long while. It gave little more
than routine help to the communists.

From 1936 onwards the main communist base was in
the thinly populated and barren north-west of China. The
area controlled by the communists was at first small; their
army, though efficient and strictly disciplined, was minute
compared with the armies of the Kuomintang; and, though
they maintained secret cells in most of the large cities, there
was little that they could usefully attempt. The total membership of the CCP in 1937 was no more than 40,000.

Nevertheless the communists survived as an organised
force, and that was to be the cause of their ultimate successes. Their adversary, Chiang Kai-shek, understood this:
hence his unremitting efforts to extirpate them. The communists had to wait. Waiting is the secret of victory in

China. Chiang Kai-shek waited at Chungking and wore out the Japanese; the communists waited at Yenan, until their time came. During this waiting period the communists fought chiefly as guerillas. Mao, and his commander-in-chief Chu-teh, summarised their military tactics as follows:

When the enemy advances, we retreat.
When the enemy halts and encamps, we trouble them.
When the enemy seeks to avoid battle, we attack.
When the enemy retreats, we pursue.[7]

By these tactics, the communists persisted; and for the Kuomintang they remained an unremovable threat.

It was foreign war—the war of China with Japan—which transformed their prospects. Japan, fearing that China was at last consolidating itself, struck at the Kuomintang. Japan had seized Manchuria in 1931. In 1937 it began full-scale war. For eight years the Kuomintang struggled against the strongest military power in Asia; its only real assets were the size of China and the general state of disorganisation in the country, which made it hard for Japan to exploit its military successes. About half of China was over-run, but the Kuomintang managed to survive, and to maintain its government from the remote inland city of Chungking. More deadly to the Kuomintang than the Japanese assault was the war-time sapping and mining by the communists. At the start of the war, a truce had been made between the Kuomintang and the communists; but it was only a nominal and the communists used the plight of the Kuomintang very skilfully in preparing the downfall of Chiang Kai-shek's regime.

They developed a deadly propaganda. They represented communism, not the Kuomintang, as the best custodian of the national interests. They spread the impression that the Kuomintang was fighting a phoney war against Japan, while the communists fought in hard earnest. Although in fact the communists fought very little, and when they did so, often fought not the Japanese but the Kuomintang, they used the war to build up communism as true nationalism.

The strain of war in the end broke the Kuomintang. Its regime, which had begun promisingly, became corrupt and inefficient almost beyond belief. When the war ended, and the Kuomintang returned to the luxuries of the coastal towns, the collapse of morale was intensified. Everything was for sale. And the Kuomintang could offer nothing for the future. It had no policy. Every month made it clearer that it never would have one.

For a short time the nominal truce with the communists was continued, and negotiations for a long-term accommodation took place through the mediation of the American General Marshall, who had been sent to China by President Truman to try to bolster up China as part of the organisation of post-war Asia. Probably neither side would have stuck by an agreement. The communists saw the Kuomintang crumbling. The time had come for them to inherit its power.

They proceeded according to Mao's strategy. They recruited much larger peasant armies, using for this purpose the grievances of the tenants against the landlord. In the end they had raised the largest peasant armies ever seen in the history of Asia. These armies spread their hold over ever larger tracts of the country. They began to cut the railway lines. Then they moved to the attack on the towns. The country was storming the cities. Finally they met and defeated the Kuomintang armies in pitched battle. Thereafter the Kuomintang regime dissolved with extraordinary speed. Its armies dispersed.* The Kuomintang was swept off the mainland, and maintained itself only in the island of Formosa.

In September 1949, Mao Tse-tung, from the gate of

---

* The small dissident parties which the Kuomintang had allowed to come into being repudiated their connection with it, and declared for communism.

Forbidden City in Peking, proclaimed the setting up of the Chinese People's Republic.

The communists were thus left masters in the country. The concepts to which they owed their success—the revolutionary army, the secure base, the encircling of the towns— were concepts of the Chinese and of Mao Tse-tung, not of the Russians. Mao had played by ear. He had proceeded experimentally. He called his revolution a communist one, but it had little to do with the marxist or leninist revolutions. More accurately it could be called a maoist revolution.

The special nature of Mao Tse-tung's practice in carrying through communist revolution stands out more clearly if it is contrasted with the no less peculiar nature of communist tactics in the Middle East. These have been analysed by Walter Laqueur in his remarkable book, *Communism and Nationalism in the Middle East*. In the countries of this area, the communist parties scarcely try at all to mobilise mass support. They do not attempt to start civil war, or to raise up peasant armies. Instead, they rely upon the communist party as being the best disciplined and best organised among the political groups. In the prevailing confusion of political life, they rely on being able to slip into office at some moment of crises; and, if they thus achieve power, they expect to be able to hold on to it.

What had been Russia's contribution to this great victory of communism? Very little. Mao had ceased to listen very attentively to Russian advice. Until the end of the war, Russia had refused to take his prospects seriously. In 1944 Stalin said so quite bluntly to an American visitor, Averell Harriman. Of course it is possible that he was disingenuous, but his actions bear out his words. True, after the war Russia gave great help to the Chinese communists by handing over to them some of the arms surrendered to them by the Japanese, and thereafter, with Mao's forces and Russia having a common border, Russian military aid increased. But even until almost the end, Russia was willing to negotiate with the Kuomintang. It never believed in the Chinese communist revolution until it had happened.

By his empirical way of making a revolution, by his breach with the Russian precedents, Mao Tse-tung offered a new pattern for imitation in Asia. Mao established himself as a master of revolution on equal terms with Lenin and Stalin. The new pattern—the Chinese pattern—was given a distinctive name. It is called the 'People's Liberation Movement'. In revolutions of this type, the distinctive mark is that, instead of proceeding chiefly by underground conspiracy carried on by a relatively small number of revolutionaries, it proceeds by raising large-scale civil war. It envisages pitched battles between armies, guerilla action across whole countries, and the total mobilisation of a large part of the nation to overturn the existing government. The question for the future was whether a 'People's Liberation Movement' was to be for China only or could be adopted elsewhere.

4

Imitating China

WAS the Chinese way to be followed elsewhere in Asia —or everywhere in Asia? To that question the Asian communists, and also the communist theorists in Moscow, were bound to address themselves after Mao's triumph. Up to the end of the second world war, active and sustained communist insurrection in Asia had been limited to China. Moscow's interest in Asia had flagged. But with the end of the war communism gathered its strength for a more serious effort throughout the Asian continent. This was because the war had brought about a revolutionary situation.

For this, the prime cause was the victories—short-lived though they were—of Japan. Their significance is still not properly grasped by westerners trying to understand Asian history. Japan has played a fateful part in the fortunes of western imperialism. By remaining unconquered in the latter part of the nineteenth century it showed that Asia need not necessarily be a victim of the West; by its victory over Russia in 1905 it gave impetus to the nationalism developing everywhere in Asia. Its own imperialist excesses were usually condoned, at least in part, for was not Japan really showing that an Asian power could be as efficient and ruthless as a European one? That is why Indian revolutionaries had so often turned towards it, right down to Subhas Bose in the last war.

Japan's victories after 1941 made the continuation of western empire in Asia virtually impossible, at least over the long run. Japan had given most of the peoples of southeast Asia the forms of political freedom, and they were not likely to revert willingly to being colonies, the more especially because the prestige of the West had been shattered. Nor was this all; Japan not only strengthened the will to be free but it left behind a situation which the returning western colonial powers found it extremely difficult to control. The war had shaken the social structure in all the countries of south-east Asia; the police and other branches of administration were disorganised; the economy for a time broken. There was poverty, misery, despair, uprooted men, cynicism about the future. Old ways and old leaders were discredited. Moreover, the Japanese (and the American) armies left behind large quantities of weapons. These were tools for revolutionaries.

Japan itself, the author of this general confusion, lay finally in even more complete collapse than the countries which it had over-run. Military defeat and savage air bombardment had destroyed it. It lay as helpless before its conquerors as did Germany.

Thus throughout Asia, except perhaps in India, Pakistan and Ceylon (which were themselves much disturbed) the situation in 1945 might have seemed ideal for communism. The wonder is that it did not try to exploit it more effectively the moment the war ended, and why more opposition was not made to the temporary reimposition of western authority. The reasons were probably twofold. First, the communist parties of Asia were not sufficiently well organised or alert to use immediately the revolutionary situation. They needed time to make their plans. Second, Moscow, under Stalin's rule, was for a time strangely indifferent to Asia. Stalin was extremely cautious. He did not wish to challenge the West where it was not necessary to do so, and he probably underestimated the extent to which western authority in Asia had already been broken.

In the first years of the peace the Asian communist parties were to a great extent left to themselves to devise tactics. One of the strangest spectacles of the times was that of many different peoples, some highly sophisticated, some comparatively ignorant, bound together in common allegiance to marxism, and groping to discover what marxism taught for the circumstances of the hour. As the communists gathered together their strength for their revolutionary effort, how could they assess their assets? One was pre-eminent. In most Asian countries there existed the nucleus of a disciplined communist party. That had been the one solid achievement of the earlier years, and it was of prime importance. The existence of a disciplined party is the indispensable condition for communist revolution. But the leaders, when they were realist, had to admit that, beyond surviving, the communist parties had done singularly little. Their activities—the penetration of trade unions, propaganda to the armed forces—had not brought them within sight of the seizure of power. Whenever they had come out into the open—in Indonesia, in Japan—they had suffered immediate defeat and near extinction. They had not been able to raise peasant armies, as Mao had done; they had not even tried to do so, and probably had not understood his achievements. Partly their failure had been due to the fact that in the colonial countries the administration and the police had until the outbreak of war with Japan continued to be resolute and formidable. They were sledge-hammers cracking a nut.

The first decisions by the communist leaders in most

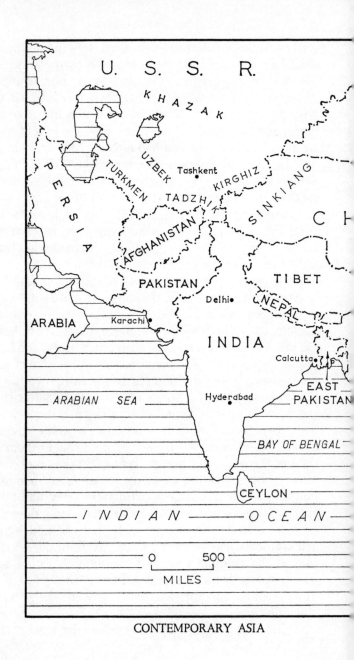

CONTEMPORARY ASIA

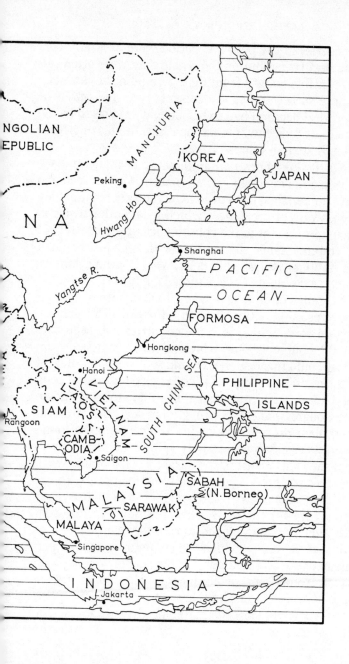

Asian countries in the post-war period were naturally confused and vacillating. But on the whole they were often surprisingly sensible, judged from their own point of view, and all the more so because of the contrast with their pre-war folly. One vital decision had to be made: what was to be the communist attitude towards nationalism, the blazing force which dominated all others in Asia?

The orthodox, metropolitan theorists of marxism have always been ambivalent about nationalism. On the one hand they have understood its power. On the other hand they have been aware of the danger which local nationalisms in the USSR might present to the continuance of the centralised Russian empire. Hence the caution with which they dealt with all national issues. This is shown in Stalin's famous little tract, *Marxism and the National Question*.

The Asian communist leaders took a rather simpler line. They regarded nationalism as a force which might be captured—a force which in some countries had been captured by the bourgeoisie but which might be snatched from them. How could this be done? Opinions differed in different countries. In India, because of peculiar circumstances, communists had drifted into sharp hostility to the Indian National Congress, and the struggle between the two was bitter and plain. In other countries, the communists found their interests best served by partly veiling their hostility to the established nationalist parties, and by collaborating with them in their struggles against the western powers. In the course of their alliance with the bourgeois nationalists, they hoped to secure for themselves key positions. On the coat tails of nationalism they hoped to ride to power.

This was the policy which the communist leaders, perhaps instinctively and without a great deal of reflection on the lessons from China or elsewhere, followed at first in Malaya, Burma, Indonesia, and in what was then still called Indochina. They were impeded by some circumstances. One was that communism tended to be identified with the

Chinese communities, so much feared in south-east Asia. Nevertheless, in some countries they began to make rapid headway. In Indochina they succeeded in gaining control of the Viet Minh (the revolutionary movement in the part of the country called Vietnam) and in turning the nationalist struggle against the French into a communist movement. In Burma it was for a time touch-and-go whether they would gain control of the Anti-Fascist Peoples Freedom League. In Malaya, because at first they announced that they would act legally they were permitted by the British government to operate openly. The Malayan Communist Party made the most of its opportunity to conduct propaganda and prepare itself for later violent action. It flooded Malaya and Singapore with communist literature. At first the party concentrated on organising trade unions, which were really so many cells and incipient soviets. Unions were set up for every type and grade of worker, from tin miners to cabaret girls; the union officers were supplied by the Malayan Communist Party, and all units were controlled by the party's General Labour Union. In 1946 a series of strikes in Singapore showed their strength. But at this period, the non-communist nationalists were still very poorly organised. Their weakness made it harder for communists to conceal themselves behind the nationalist mask. The activity was seen to be communist pure and simple.

A better example of communist co-operation with nationalists is Indonesia. There the genuine non-communist nationlists had been able to proclaim and organise a government during the last phase of the Japanese occupation. The struggle between this government and the Dutch, who tried to resume their control, was long and complex. In the course of it, the communists collaborated with the nationalists for more than two years. They used the opportunity which this gave them to worm their way into the key organisations. They gained control of the leadership of the principal trade union federation, the SOBSI, and affiliated it to the World Federation of Trade Unions. In order to improve their own position in the governing coalition, and to weaken that of the right wing nationalists, they organised a 'People's Democratic Front', which included left wing socialists. During all this time, some of the leading members of the Indonesian Communist Party successfully hid their party membership and foisted themselves on left wing groups as socialists. One of them, Amir Sjarifuddin, who had been secretly a party member since 1935, even managed for a time to become prime minister. The general aim was to build up in secret a conspiratorial organisation which at the proper moment would be able, with a minimum of effort, to crush the right wing nationalists and take over the new state for communism.

Similarly in the Philippines, the communist party penetrated, and eventually took over, a radical national organisation called the Hukbalahaps which had been formed for opposing the Japanese. In Burma also the communists hoped at first to capture the non-communist national front.

These tactics were very similar to those of the communists in China in the years when they tried to penetrate and seize the Kuomintang. In south-east Asia the struggle against western imperialism served the same purpose as the North Expedition in giving point to the alliance.

By the end of 1947, an observer who understood the realities of Asia might have assumed that the 'boring and mining' tactics of communism were proving distinctly effective. Progress had of course been uneven. It was slowest in India. But, given time, the communists might have expected in some countries—Indonesia especially—to be eventually in a position to throw off the mask and to seize power. They were frustrated by intervention from outside.

Moscow intervened. Russia had become once again interested in Asia. It was no longer diffident about challenging the West in its colonies. True, it still failed to grasp that the

West was leaving Asia, and that a continental revolution was taking place. It assumed that the West was trying to camouflage its empires by converting them into new forms. It wanted to strike at them while the transition was in progress. Moreover, this was elsewhere a time of militant communist expansion, of the Zhdanov policies, of the coup in Czechoslovakia and the Berlin blockade. In Asia, the Chinese communists had shown what might be done by open civil war. Their example could no longer be neglected.

A new wind was blowing, the wind of insurrection, of the bid for immediate power, of staking all on the bold and open throw.

It is usually assumed that, after decisions had been taken in Moscow, the signal for a concerted communist assault in Asia was given at a Youth Congress in Calcutta, held between February 19 and February 26, 1948. In fact, even today there is little absolute evidence about what happened at this conference. It is rumoured that a full report of its proceedings reached the prime minister of Burma, U Nu; but if this was so, he has never made it public. Its importance was quite overlooked at the time by the government under whose nose it was held. Yet what has become known since is consistent with the story that, under the cover of a more or less innocuous festival of left wing youth, there was a convention of the principal leaders of the communist parties in south Asia, and that they agreed there upon the general lines of the communist program. How far the lessons from China were assessed or discussed is obscure. But the decision was for revolt. In all countries there was to be an all-out, violent attack upon the established government. Demonstrations, strikes and ultimately civil war were to be the means used.

Whether or not this conference was decisive, a new phase in communist history began soon after it was held. It was the period of armed rising. It included many events over a great area in south Asia, the most striking of which were the communist rebellions in Malaya and Burma, the war of the Hukbalahaps in the Philippines, the Andhra rebellion in India, the civil war in Indochina, and the attempted revolution in Indonesia. The communists struck indiscriminately at the remaining colonial governments—as in Malaya—and at the new national governments which had replaced the western empires.

In south Asia, the decisive country, the centre of power and the model which influences all the lesser countries, is India. Actually India was less shaken by the communist insurrection than the lands of south-east Asia. But because of India's position, the story of the communist campaign there and of its failure is especially instructive. It has to be studied in detail.

With what forces and prospects did the Indian communists enter on the rising of 1948? The party had slowly grown in size. Just before the war it had begun to attract young men in the universities and especially the sons and daughters of some of the high-placed Indian civil servants and rich capitalists. These were young people with sick consciences and with an intellectual interest in the doctrines of marxism. Some of them gained attention by living in rather ostentatious austerity in a kind of communist barracks or secular monastery. Then came the war, which was a forcing house for all luxuriant political growths. At first, communism spread. But then, when Russia came into the war, the Indian Communist Party found itself obliged to support the war effort of the British government—being instructed to do so by Moscow—and this brought it into collision with the India National Congress, which after 1942 was in what it described as 'open rebellion' against the government and the war effort. For Indian communism this was disastrous. It had allied itself with the 'anti-national' cause. Even today it has not yet sloughed off the stigma.

How gravely it had handicapped itself was not at first understood by the Indian communist leaders. Immediately after the war they were fairly optimistic about their prospects. The war had caused great economic hardship: the Bengal famine was its most calamitous manifestation. The war brought also a stir of political excitement which culminated in the withdrawal of Britain from India, the partition of the sub-continent, and the ghastly communal riots. Economic suffering and political confusion: these were conditions apparently ideal for communist strategy.

When the decision for armed rising was taken in 1948, the communist campaign took two forms. The communists organised strikes and violence in the great cities, especially Calcutta. That was the old style of conspiracy. But in a small part of south India, the district of Telingana, they tried for a time to follow methods more like those of Mao Tse-tung. Conditions here were usually suitable because of a breakdown of ordinary administration during the trouble which followed on the refusal of the muslim state of Hyderabad to federate with the Indian Union. Indian military action was necessary in order to compel it. The communists began to raise an Indian communist army in the jungle, and tried to set up a shadow communist administration.

An interesting picture of the state of affairs in this district during the troubles exists in a novel written by an Indian, a reflective and observant civil servant, who knew well the affected areas and travelled in them during the worst of the trouble. One of the villagers arrested by the police described his experience.

We were peaceful, law-abiding folk who never troubled the government or the police. One dark night, three months ago, we were awakened by gunfire and came out of our houses to see what was the matter. The lanes of our village were lit up as bright as day, for the house was ablaze. And what did we see by the light of the fire? We saw half a dozen men carrying guns, with masks over their faces who had tied the Patwari and the Patel to posts and were flogging them, and they were also beating the Bania and these three were crying ay-ay-ay.* What could we do? The raiders had guns, and we had no guns for we were quiet, law-abiding folk. Then these raiders asked us for donations for the Communist Party. What could we do but give them money? If we had refused they would have beaten us. Then they made speeches about freedom and hoisted a red flag, and made us all salute it. Of course we saluted it. What else could we do? Then they ordered all the men to follow them to the next village, where they did likewise. Perhaps some of us did loot a little there. What else could we do? They had taken from us everything we had, so we took a little from our neighbours. And the men with guns watched to see we did not run back home. Then there was a great noise of shots, and whistles, and shouting, and the police rushed upon us and arrested us all. The men with guns ran away, but how could we run away, with houses and families to look after? So we are locked up in jail while the men with guns are still at liberty.[1]

The writer describes how during this time the officials of the government took to giving various areas a wide berth. The communist bands moved more or less safely, entered villages and murdered or maimed unpopular money-lenders. He came upon one of these groups in a forest.

We came to a place where many men were sitting round camp fires. They seemed astonished to see us, but none of them made any attempt to stop us. The sentry we had seen, and several other khaki-clad young men, seemed to be ex-soldiers. Several had a smattering

* The Patwari and Patel are minor officials. The Bania is a money-lender.

58

of English. There were about fifty men, armed with modern rifles. Many were mere boys, who ought to have been at school. There were men from other parts of the country, including a sadhu. They seemed to have introduced a regular system of conscription. Every household had to provide one man for their service, on pain of having the house looted and burned.[2]

For a time it might have seemed that here was the nucleus of something like the Chinese Red Army. If communism had taken control of a larger area, the Congress government which had succeeded the British Raj might have been shaken. But in 1948 the Indian rising could not succeed, even if it had had a leader of genius like Mao Tse-tung. The reason was that the conditions which Mao had said were necessary did not then exist in India. The base—Telingana—was too small. It was insecure. And the national government was too strong, too well organised, and enjoyed too much prestige, since it was accepted as being more truly 'national' than the communists. It was easy for it to bring great force upon the rebellion from outside; and the ordinary administration was presently restored.

Thus the Indian rebellion failed. It came to an end when the faction in the Indian party which favoured 'activism' lost face because of the failures.

In the meanwhile, similar armed insurrections had been taking place in most of the countries of south-east Asia. In Burma and Malaya, the communists had taken to the jungles and carried on guerilla war. In Indochina—where open and armed rebellion had begun in December 1946—the communists raised the Viet Minh army and made a military assault upon the government. In Indonesia they attempted a coup d'état. In the Philippines there was guerilla war. But as in India the insurrections lost their impetus, failed to achieve their main objects, except in northern Indochina, and slowly petered out. The bloodshed, self-sacrifices by youth and material havoc availed communism very little.

In Burma, after the communist guerillas had gained control of broad sections of the country, the government gradually restored its authority. The Burmese army remained dependable, and the people as a whole gave it the necessary support. The Indian government from the background supplied arms at a critical moment. In Indonesia, the communists failed to subvert the new national government which replaced Dutch rule; their major attempt at a coup was suppressed completely; as in India, the appeal of nationalism outweighed that of communism.

In the Philippines the guerilla rebellion slowly died out. Ramón Magsaysay, at first defence minister and later president, outplayed the communist leaders in political skill. In Malaya, even if the communists caused the maximum embarrassment to the government, they failed to establish their authority over any area large enough to provide them with a secure base. The government forces, even if harried by elusive attackers, were able to keep them on the move. It was impossible for the communists to create anything like a communist government or to raise forces with which to storm the urban centres. The country was too small for the kind of operations which Mao had postulated as necessary for success by his methods. The Malayan communists came to recognise this geographical factor as one of the main reasons for their unsuccess. One of their documents, captured by the government, points out that in a small country like Malaya, 'criss-crossed by a network of roads and railways', the government could discover and attack at any moment the rear bases of the communists.[3] Thus the communist effort was limited to guerilla action. It was vexatious and costly to the government, but it was never a deadly threat. The Malayan Communist Party was moreover handicapped because it was a Chinese party, and was regarded with distrust by the Malays, who saw in the communist movement an attempt to establish the rule of Chinese over Malays.

Only in Indochina did the communist attack on south-east Asia prosper. And even there the communist success, which was to result in the setting up of a communist state in northern Indochina, did not come about during the main period of activism. It was the result of six more years of persistent struggle and it happened only because China had a common border with Indochina and because the Viet Minh was able to evict the French frontier forces and to open communication with the Chinese. These reinforced the local Viet Minh communists with lavish military supplies; without Chinese help, they could not have succeeded. This was one way in which the Viet Minh struggle differed from that of the other communist countries in south-east Asia. But there was another also. The Viet Minh communists came nearer than any other to imitating the strategy of Mao Tse-tung. They were able to raise a peasant army because, after they had carved out an area for themselves on the Chinese border, they were able to operate from a secure base.

Indochina was not enough to compensate for the reverses and disappointments. The failures, when they became obvious and were admitted, set off a new and vigorous debate in communist parties everywhere about the techniques of making a revolution.

One of the results was that, without any clear proclamation of changed intentions, the communists in some of the countries of south Asia began to show more interest in the possibilities of constitutional action. In India they became sedulous parliamentarians; in the central assembly at Delhi they form the official opposition. In Indonesia, where the clemency of the government allowed them to reconstitute their organisation after their military defeat and to act as a constitutional party, they canvassed vigorously, and in the general election of 1955 obtained a very large parliamentary vote.

Nevertheless, the capital issue which continued to interest communists was the reason for the failure of the great insurrection. The defeat suffered by the communists in south-east Asia contrasted glaringly with the success won in China. Naturally it was asked whether Mao Tse-tung and the Chinese communists had a secret or a method or a plan different from that of communists elsewhere. Should the 'Chinese way' be adopted? With the prestige which came from their own victory, the Chinese, joining in the debate, had begun to speak more authoritatively in their statements about their own achievements. Their theorist, Liu Shao-chi, now head of state, had made uncompromising claims.

> The road taken by the Chinese people in defeating imperialism and in founding the Chinese People's Republic is the road that should be taken by the people's democracy. This road is the road of Mao Tse-tung. It can also be the basic road for liberation of peoples of other colonial and semi-colonial countries, where similar conditions exist.[4]

In June, 1950, just before the start of the Korean war, Peking had gone even further. It said that the lessons of the Chinese revolution applied to many colonial and semi-colonial countries outside Asia. It referred especially—and ominously—to the Middle East, Africa and Latin America.

These claims by the Chinese were naturally not very welcome to the communist leaders elsewhere, especially as they came at a time when their efforts were meeting with humiliating unsuccess. They were challenged by the communist party of India. Between the party in China and the party in India there had been for a long time little contact and some evident rivalry. India communists had been accustomed previously to expect guidance not from any Asian source, but from communists in Britain, and it was through this channel that they had received by relay the advice of Moscow. The Indians, in their turn, had aspired to advise some of the parties of south-east Asia. They were very sensitive about being eclipsed by the Chinese.

The approval of Moscow was what mattered. In the immediate post-war period, Zhukov, laying down the official Russian view, had said that the hope of the communist world in Asia lay jointly with China and India. Later the CPSU was to claim that it had 'never agreed' with Liu Shao-chi's advocacy of liberation struggles; and perhaps it pretended to do so at the time only because it was engaged in delicate negotiations with the CCP. But by the time of the Calcutta Youth Congress, China was in the ascendant. The Chinese had been crowned by success, and the Indians could hardly object. When, however, the Chinese began to lecture the rest of Asia upon theory, the Indians took their stand. They pointed out publicly—which no other communists had done—that whatever the triumph which the Chinese had won, their theory—the very theory which had won them victory—was extremely heterodox. It was the opposite of marxism and leninism. Ranadive, a rather mercurial person, who had seized the leadership of the Indian party by accusing his predecessor of being too tame, turned upon Mao some of the combativeness which he had formerly used upon the Indian government and upon opposing factions in the Indian party.

We must state emphatically that the Indian Communist Party has accepted Marx, Engels, Lenin and Stalin as the authoritative sources of Marxism. It has not discovered new sources of Marxism beyond these. Nor for the matter of that is there any Communist party which declares adherence to the so-called theory of New Democracy alleged to be propounded by Mao, and declares it to be a new addition to Marxism. It must be admitted that some of Mao's formulations are such that no Communist party can accept them; they are in contradiction to the world understanding of the Communist parties. Those who contrast the Chinese and Russian way have many things wrong in their minds. First, their idea about the Russian revolution is wrong. They think that the Russian revolution was achieved suddenly on November 7—a one-day show, a sort of coup—and forget the dogged fight for three decades, the persistent effort to win over the majority of the people during the revolution and before. They also forget the civil war. Secondly, when they contrast and uphold what they call the Chinese way they seek to reject the hegemony of the proletariat in the democratic revolution and feel that the Chinese revolution shows that the hegemony of the proletariat is not necessary.[5]

This article in the Bombay journal *Communist* appeared in June 1949. For the next few months sharp exchanges took place between the Indian and Chinese parties. They became a scandal among the communists. Finally, international communism intervened, and in January 1950, the Cominform—successor to the Comintern—publicly instructed the Indian party to conform to the Chinese view.

The Indians held out for another six months, then capitulated. They confessed that they had slandered Mao. They recanted and admitted that Mao was a true leninist and stalinist, and that their own opposed views had been a 'full-fledged' trotskyite thesis. They asked that their previous views should be entirely cancelled and no longer regarded as authoritative.

Yet that was not the end. A year later, Moscow itself had second thoughts about Chinese claims. After all, if

China was to lay down the law for all communist Asia, and if its revolution was to be accepted as the standard Asian pattern, the Russian government might well fear for the future of its prestige on the Asian continent, and for its own share of the leadership in promoting revolution. A discreet reduction of China's claim was to be expected. It came in the form of a statement by a group of Soviet orientalists who in November 1951 met in Moscow and defined the Russian view. 'The experience of the Chinese revolution', they said, 'is of immense significance. But it would be risky to regard the Chinese revolution as some kind of stereotype for peoples' democratic revolutions in other parts of Asia.'[6]

After that, Peking tactfully gave up its references to a Chinese way for India. The accepted communist view was that it is the task of each national party to find for itself the best means of seizing power. At this period, communist propaganda in all countries spoke of China, and of Mao, with regard; but it depicted China less as the apostle of a new-style revolution than as a strong territorial state, the secure base from which communism could radiate. Communist parties in the rest of Asia were not instructed to follow Mao's methods of seizing power.

Nevertheless all Asian communists looked increasingly to China for diplomatic offensive to reduce the will and strength of Asian governments to suppress their communist oppositions. In a little while, the support was to become much more vigorous.

The conclusion drawn from these events by outside observers was fairly comforting. A dangerous communist plan to gain power by quiet penetration had been spoiled by the impetuousness of communist leadership; and the heart of the failure seemed to be in Moscow. Until the decision was made to resort to armed insurrection, the communist parties in most of the countries of free Asia had been prospering by their quiet methods of boring from within. Given time and a continuance of these tactics, communism might have had a fair chance of coming to power in one country or another, if it waited patiently until a conjuncture occurred when, by dropping its disguises and striking suddenly, it might take over authority virtually by surprise. But communism in the time of the ascendency of Zhdanov was not patient. Years of careful work were in consequence destroyed.

Yet what had happened once might happen again, and the fomenting and planning might be undertaken, not by Russia, but by an increasing militant China. This was in the minds of those who, at the start of the 1950s, refused to rejoice in the assumption that the communist threat was finally lifted from Asia.

5

The New Asian Power

IT is now necessary to retrace our steps a little, to the moment in 1949 when the communists had set up their government at Peking. From this new base, their vision was enlarged and new vistas opened to them for the spread of communist, or Chinese, power.

Communist or Chinese: which was it to be? It is from the overlap, the lack of distinction and yet the contradictions between these two imperatives that have come many of the paradoxes and uncertainties of Chinese policy. China has had double aims, a double foreign policy, a double ambition; and this has made it very hard for other powers to come to terms with it. This factor has also made it a difficult and exacting ally for Russia—though in Russia's case this dual role of China's should have been understandable by Moscow, for it is very much akin to the role which the Soviet Union has discharged since the October revolution.

On the one hand, the Soviet Union has been the agent of the communist movement and has tried to spread communist revolution throughout the world, thereby confronting the pragmatic nationalist statesmen of Europe with a maddening universalism which has led Moscow to interfere where no Russian national interests were at stake. On the other hand, the Soviet Union has continued to be a national state. It is the heir of Holy Russia, and as such has cultivated national interests which have often been narrow and prone to negate the objectives of international communism. Sometimes this has been so evident that some of the leaders of the CPSU have revolted and thrown down the gauntlet to the bureaucrats who guide the Russian state. In the resulting battle of wills they have not infrequently been defeated.

This pattern was to be repeated in China. But at first the duality was hidden. The Chinese government fulfilled the two roles without the contradiction between them becoming glaringly apparent. As the leaders of the new regime looked out from Peking, they were aware of one essential fact: Chinese communism was lapped round by waves of anti-communism. All the world was hostile; in making head against this hostility, China both improved the prospects of success of world communism and also laid the foundations for a revival of the National Chinese Empire.

The Chinese leaders made a distinction, however, between the smaller nation states of Asia—which they regarded with the hauteur traditional to their country—and the much more formidable power of America, operating from afar and largely through the smaller nations of Asia. America had its hand on the very heart of China: it was the patron of Chiang Kai-shek. To overcome this 'two Chinas' division and to expel American influence from the Chinese nation became the guiding motive of the new regime's policy. The fixity of its intention became almost a mania; but it was fundamentally rational and understandable. Chiang Kai-shek was the old regime still in being, and the communists dreaded lest, given time and enough American help, he might enlarge himself to become a sufficient threat to topple them down from their thrones in Peking. Hence their opposition to compromise proposals for recognising two Chinas: a communist mainland and a nationalist Formosa. All China was one, they said, and could not exist partly communist and partly Kuomintang. But the reason for their tenacity on this point was the determination to deny the United States a foothold in China. American influence must be expelled root and branch. This required the elimination of Chiang Kai-shek.

The United States also intervened in Asia, and hence in the immediate sphere of Chinese concern, by its patronage of small nations existing on the fringes of China. It was the champion of their independence, and at the same time held that this independence was consistent with such countries' affording military facilities to America of direct value to its plans for containing communism. China at first, therefore, was hostile towards these nations. Subsequently it contended for the support of Asian nationalism against the United States. Its aim has been to ensure that the United States, under the guise of acting as protector of small nations, should not acquire bases by means of which China would be deprived of freedom of action.

But why should the government in Peking, from the start, have regarded the United States as its sworn enemy, apparently ruling out all possibility of reaching an understanding with America? China's communist leaders were not inclined to respond to any generous and imaginative gesture unless assured of its validity by America's surrendering completely its position in the Far East. And this America was unlikely to do. For several decades, the United States had been an active power in the Pacific and had thought of itself, with some justice, as the champion of progressive causes—above all of nationalism. Victor in the greatest war in history, it was not likely to bow before a parvenu government in China and to withdraw from what it conceived to be its liberalising role in Asia. If in the first months after the communist triumph in China its resolution seemed somewhat pliant, it was goaded into inflexibility by the insults from Peking and the apparent madness of everything that came out of China. Peking, far from offering a dialogue with the outer world, conducted a hysterical monologue against it.

In committing itself to so aggressive a posture, China was at first satisfied that Russia, the senior apostle of the communist faith, was its sure ally. Russia, it is true, was then under Stalin, and the relations of the Chinese communists with Stalin were admittedly curious and complex. Stalin was a difficult cross for them to bear: more than once they had found that, in pursuit of his own national designs, Stalin had been willing to betray, or at best disregard, Chinese communism. Its victory in China he had obviously considered to be of little worth to him. He apparently reckoned that the interests of Russia were better served by a weak Kuomintang government, which he could dominate and bully and have fawning on him, than by a communist regime which, if only because of its ideological character and self-justified pride, could stand up to him. Indeed, there is evidence that Stalin would have liked a Kuomintang China, from which the peripheral provinces could be detached and made to serve as buffer states for the Soviet Union. This would seem to have been the motive of Russia's sponsorship of the Republic of East Turkestan in 1944, of the occupation of Inner Mongolia by Soviet-officered troops from Outer Mongolia (which would have resulted in the creation of a united Mongolia if the Chinese communists had not triumphed), and, though less clearly, of the plan to create a communist satellite in northern Manchuria in 1946. However, with Mao's triumph, the situation had, willy nilly, changed. Chinese communism was an established fact, an outstanding success. Russia surely would greet it with friendship and respect.

The Chinese asked two things of the Soviet Union. One was material help—capital and technical assistance—to enable China to develop itself as rapidly as possible and become strong, while having as little as possible to do with the United States and the capitalist world. The other was to guard its rear. This Russia virtually was constrained to do: all the geopolitical considerations impelled it; it was unthinkable that Russia should decline the task. And with Russia guaranteeing the security and tranquillity of its frontiers in the central land-mass of Asia, China was free to think and act, and to plot against all the miscellaneous countries and interests which blocked its progress in the world.

For action and plotting, the new government at Peking was ideally situated. Its spirit was radically different from that of the Kuomintang. It had a mission other than of surviving in a hostile world. An elixir of exuberance coursed through the veins of this reunited, reinvigorated China which now confidently looked outwards for new worlds to conquer. the government had ready in its service a million or more ardent party workers—cadres or *kanpus*—who could be persuaded to apply themselves to any task, no matter what hardship it imposed on them. Chinese communism was not content with pacifying its own people and establishing an efficient, workable system; it set itself with calm deliberation to stir up hell in Asia. Wherever revolution promised, China would be at hand to promote it; wherever revolution led, it would follow.

Its first adventure came in Korea. On the borders of Manchuria, Korea existed in partitioned form as the result of an accident of wartime occupation. North Korea, under Russian control, was communist; the South was nationalist and, being under American influence, was a notable example of a fringe-territory on the Chinese borderland likely to give harbour to American bases. The nationalism of the South was therefore the enemy to be overcome.

But it was Russia which took the initiative, and did so

without apparently either consulting or informing China beforehand. In June 1950 it impelled North Korea—which certainly would not have dared undertake such an operation without the assent, or rather the command, of Russia —to launch a campaign, with armies, airplanes and all the equipment of full-scale military aggression, against the South.

This was Russia's solitary attempt to spread communism by a straightforward military offensive. It is still a mystery why an essentially cautious man like Stalin emboldened himself to take the military offensive against what he must have recognised as an American sphere of influence. It is possible that he had miscalculated America's intentions. American speeches at this time were listing the territories which America would go to war to defend: Korea was conspicuously omitted. Stalin may have concluded that the United States would back down if there were a determined communist drive, that it would give way in a situation where aggression could be checked only at the risk of a major war. But if this was Stalin's expectation, he was disappointed. It may indeed have been the original intention of the American administration not to take up the Soviet challenge, but if so, it was over-ruled by President Truman. Russia's intelligence service may have correctly reported American military thinking on the question, but it had not correctly estimated the attitude of the civilian president. By adroit use of international procedures, Truman organised a United Nations military operation to defend South Korea and provided American strength with which to do so. It was the Soviet Union which withdrew from the conflict, not the United States.

With Russia in retreat, China stepped forward. The American and allied armies, flying the United Nations flag, were met by Chinese armies. The government in Peking (acting with a certain prudence and willing to keep the conflict to a limited war if America also would abstain from full-scale war) proclaimed these troops to be 'volunteers'. They were, according to Peking, 'irregular forces' operating of their own free will, without committing the Chinese government. China and America clashed with startling force, and Korea became one of the most fought-over and devastated regions of the world. In this conflict, the Chinese army, so little regarded until then, showed itself utterly transformed; thenceforth Chinese military prestige was a major factor. At the same time, China learned beyond doubt that American power was a reality, not a 'paper tiger', and that there were limits beyond which China would be ill advised to go. The war ended in an uneasy truce, with the frontier between North and South Korea in the same position as it had been when the fighting began. But the South was protected by the certainty that the United States would return to action if it were again attacked.

As a result of the war, a fierce factional contest was waged between the pro-Chinese and the pro-Russian communists in North Korea. Many of the details of this contest are excessively obscure. In so far as any light can be shed on them, it is through the personality and career of Kim Il-sung, the head of the North Korean government. He had begun his career as a Russian officer. He was jobbed into the leadership by the engaging sleight-of-hand of giving him the name of a deceased national leader against Japan who had been prominent twenty years before; presumably this attracted popular support, and hence power, to him. For a time, Kim was content to lead the pro-Russian party, but he seems to have quarrelled with the Russians after the Korean war was over and to have changed sides. As a convinced stalinist, he dislikes Khrushchev so much that he now sides with the Chinese. The relations of Peking with this client state on its borders have become the pattern of what China desires to establish everywhere. Today, as the result of years of diplomacy, Peking seems to be bringing about something of the same relationship with Burma and Indonesia. But elsewhere

Peking's 'client state' policy has still far to develop.

Another arena of activity for China during this period—the immediate aftermath of the communist party's victory—was Japan. Here the activist stage was brief. Communist strategy in Japan followed different lines from elsewhere: activism was an aberration. The situation in Japan was remarkably unrewarding for violent action. But Japan's political alignment was akin to that of other Asian nations, and this for China was ample justification for an interventionist policy. As the result of war and occupation by the United States, Japan and its new liberal institutions were safeguarded by American power. That power was thereby entrenched in Asia, and it threatened China. At first, before Peking had learned patience, it used every opportunity to shake the Japanese tree violently.

In the first years after the second world war, the communist party in Japan was the most faction-ridden in the world. Sometimes the party heeded Moscow, sometimes Peking. The group led by Tokuda—a fiery personality from the outer islands—burned for dramatic action. It was at feud with the group led by Nosaka which sought to charm the Japanese people into supporting communism by giving the party a benign face. At the time of the Korean war, the Tokuda faction came to the top and resorted to violence. In this it probably was paying more attention to the signals and commands coming from Moscow than to those emanating from Peking.

This campaign of violence was short and ineffective. It was limited to organising some rather spectacular demonstrations and riots, and to training squads of rioters in the country districts. In the circumstances obtaining in Japan, the communist leaders could not hope to raise a Red Army, to carve out a secure base, or to imitate in any way the successful policy of Mao Tse-tung. If Japan were ever to go communist, it would not do so by its communists' imitating the methods of China.

While engaged in the Korean war, China had also for the first time collided with India, the other government which commanded a vast stretch of the Asian mainland. India had recently emancipated itself from Britain and was in a rather exalted mood. Its government was prepared to welcome China as a nation with a destiny similar to its own: an Asian giant, renascent after many decades of humiliation by the West. It saw China in international terms as a great Asian state rather than in ideological categories of communist and non-communist.

But for China the picture was quite different. Its leaders did not believe in the reality of the Indian revolution or that India had really freed itself from Britain and become a sovereign and independent power; rather, they saw communism as the eventual destiny of India, though when this should come about might still be uncertain. In the meantime, the Chinese communists looked on India's independence as a cunning sleight-of-hand by Britain: the working out of a modernised formula of imperialism which would subordinate India more effectually than civil servants and military forces had been able to do in the past. Worse: India might be expected to afford bases not only to Britain—which the Chinese had come to regard as an obsolescent power—but to America, whose power China was feeling so heavily in Korea. It is perhaps not surprising, therefore, that the Chinese were unresponsive to India's offer of friendship.

The first occasion of a clash between the two countries was over Tibet in 1950. China's government courted the collision. India was hurt and surprised. Having taken possession of the central government of China, the communists were setting about repossessing the territories traditionally held by China when its government was powerful. One of these territories was Tibet. The Tibetans are quite different from the Chinese in race, language, way of life and religious outlook. Any union between the two can only be superficial and maintainable only by force. When there is a strong power radiating from the central government in China, Tibet becomes a subject province. By the degree of autonomy enjoyed by Tibet, the strength of China at a given time may be measured. When it is feeble, Lhasa is an independent entity; when strong, Lhasa ceases to be an important factor politically.

The period of the eclipse of Chinese strength was coming to an end by 1950, and with it Tibetan freedom. But the Tibetans, in asserting their independence at the turn of the twentieth century, had involved their destiny with that of India, which, at the time when Chinese influence was at its nadir, was under British control. Autonomous Tibet had come to enjoy the approval of the government of India.* Based on the Himalayan border, British power loomed and watched over Tibet benevolently. This role, and various treaty rights on which it was based, were inherited by the government of independent India.

The Chinese government had to decide how to deal with Indian objections to the full restoration of Chinese control. It did not hesitate. In October 1950 it sent its army into Tibet, brushing aside two Indian protests, and forced on the Dalai Lama a treaty recognising that Tibet was an integral part of China. All that India could do on the Dalai Lama's behalf was to get written into the treaty a mild provision to the effect that the Tibetan way of life was to be allowed to continue.

This reduction of Tibet, this lack of resistance to the first powerful bid to restore China's historic frontiers, was a critical moment in Asia's history. As so often happens, many of those charged with responsibility were not fully

---

* Britain was at times tempted to annex Tibet, but found it more convenient that Tibet should be a buffer state between China and India than that it should be a part of the British empire.

aware of what they were doing, and took grave steps without realising the consequences. As George Meredith says: the sky is often blue and the air untroubled when the Rubicon is crossed. The two men most responsible for India's tolerating the Chinese advance into Tibet were the prime minister, Jawaharlal Nehru, and Sardar Panikkar, the Indian ambassador in Peking. They saw that China really meant what it said and was ready to use force for the reoccupation of a territory traditionally regarded by China as belonging to it, and that India would have to use force if it wished to defend its own recently acquired rights there. This India's government was not willing to do. In the circumstances it was hardly possible. How would India, which aspired to the role of the champion of nationalism everywhere, have shown itself to the world if it had gone to war with China: a country which, though communist, was more conspicuous in the eyes of most people in Asia and elsewhere as a resurgent Asian nation?

Tibet, moreover, lay beyond India's Himalayan frontiers and could not effectively be secured by the Indian army. The idea that it could do so was ludicrous, as must have been made clear by the Indian General Staff, if this was consulted. The government's military advisers would have had grave anxiety for any Indian troops which pushed beyond the Himalayan frontier. That this was never seriously contemplated is shown by the fact that Nehru could make the momentous surrender in Tibet—with consequences in the ensuing years which must have been at least partly foreseeable—and yet have only two or three persons in the Indian parliament oppose him. There was a wholly inadequate discussion of the problem in the Indian press. As happens so often in history, the crisis had arrived, and the majority of intelligent people did not recognise it as such. For nearly a decade after 1950, India went on saluting its Asian 'partner', admiring its achievements, and elaborating the idea of what great things might be done if the two countries put themselves jointly at the head of Asia. For a time, Indian national opinion was in love with the idea of China's rising in its new strength, and saw the regime in Peking through coloured spectacles which filtered out all the unlovely aspects of its communism. Actively wooing China, India refused to be rebuffed by the coldness, contempt and derision with which the new Chinese communists treated the new Indian state in the early years of their regime.*

India, motivated thus, surrendered all rights in Tibet inherited from the British—rights to maintain troops in the country, rights to operate telegraphs—and threw its influence against any effective response by the United Nations when Tibet appealed there. Only San Salvador and Ireland took up Tibet's case. China thereby extended its control of Asia, and was in a position, when it chose, to pursue an active frontier policy along the border between India and Tibet, which was now the border between India and China: an area which for so long had virtually ceased to be of serious concern to India.†

* India's problem was a little like that of France and England when Germany reoccupied the Rhineland in 1936. Only, India had definite reasons for thinking that China really would use force, whereas we now know that Hitler was bluffing and would have retreated if he had run into determined opposition.

† After suppressing Tibetan independence, China undertook, at first tentatively and then, a few years later, more resolutely, a campaign against the indigenous institutions of Tibet. It pushed through something akin to the dissolution of the monasteries in sixteenth-century England. This led to much suffering and was certainly against the will of the Tibetan people. But in the absence of competent or reliable press reporting, it has been difficult to assess the degree of persecution involved. Statements in the Dalai Lama's book, *My Land and My People* (London and New York, 1962) and in the report of the International Commission of Jurists (*Tibet and The Chinese People's Republic*, Geneva, 1960), may be entirely accurate, but they cannot be taken as first hand evidence. It is worth noting that the Chinese, while moving strongly against the political mani-

It is possible to watch China at this period learning as it practised its foreign policy. The early policy, immediately after the establishment of the communist regime, is crude and uninformed; the later policy is marked by shrewdness and insight.

The important fact which Chinese communism learned from the Korean war was the value to it of the neutralist sentiment of Asia, particularly of its leading exponent, India. The more sharp-sighted amongst the diplomatists in the party realised that, absurd as India's unrequited love might seem, India's actions, India's delusions, India's disinterestedness could be made into powerful instruments for China's foreign policy. Throughout the Korean war and during the prolonged wrangles between China and America in coming to terms over the armistice, India had been of the greatest use to China, whether as diplomatic courier, as the non-aligned power able to act as a genuine third party, or as the amenable friend who could be induced to fly kites on Peking's behalf. India had played a most important role in modifying the attitude of the United Nations when there seemed a danger of the Korean war's escalating into something much larger; and it is not extravagant to say that India had been the shield between China and a much more serious military effort by the United States. In the latter phases of negotiation, it was only India's participation in the scheme which made it possible to get agreement to a plan for resolving the complex dispute over the repatriation of prisoners.

Chou En-lai in particular, who at this time was the shaper of China's foreign policy, gave due weight to the value of good relations with India. With Tibet now in

festations of buddhism, have at the same time patronised the elements of buddhism in Chinese culture and history. Apparently the official view is that China derived much glory from its relation with buddhism in the past, and the government has attempted to revive Chinese reputation for scholarship in buddhist studies.

China's hands and the Korean war a 'drawn game' enhancing China's prestige, Chou prepared a momentous change of front in Chinese foreign policy. The zeal of India to be of service was now to be given free rein, and China would pay the necessary price. The outer world was no longer to be regarded as uniformly hostile. Hostility was now graded in shades, and India was found to be almost sparklingly white in comparison with the black which was America. In other words, under Chou's guidance China grew suddenly mature in foreign policy (though the maturity had constantly to be striven for, and the old intransigent attitude was apt to break through at the least provocation), and was prepared to play a subtle game of advancing its interests by siding with certain powers against others. China had become like other powers in the world— like Russia itself—and even though its long-term intentions remained as crusading and maximalist as ever, it seemed to the outside world that China was becoming a more tolerable power to deal with.

The official Chinese 'line' on India changed noticeably after the Tibetan invasion of 1950. The Congress revolution was no longer dismissed as a fraud. Gandhi, the father of the Indian nation, was transferred from the pillory reserved for arch-hypocrites and deceivers of the people to an honoured niche in the pantheon of Asia's leaders. Jawaharlal Nehru ceased to be 'the running dog of imperialism'.

Nehru in fact proved himself of almost incalculable value during this stage. The campaign of John Foster Dulles to organise the independent countries of Asia into a crusade against China goaded Nehru into a counter-crusade to keep these countries unattached. He had a very considerable amount of success, for non-alignment touched something very deep in the Asian heart, and struck a responsive chord in Asian ambitions. Why should any Asian country, which should be concentrating on its own national problems, allow itself to be manipulated by the United States for purposes in which American interests might be involved but which seemed remote from Asian concern?

The Asian states responded to India's diplomatic lead, and though this was complicated by all kinds of tensions, old vendettas and jealousies, it was triumphantly expressed in the Bandung Conference of the Afro-Asian powers held in 1955. The conference, one of the most colourful of the post-war era, was really more of a demonstration for neutralism than a meeting for negotiation. Opinion running counter to the general trend was not obliterated, and managed to express itself, but on the whole the forefront of the stage was taken by the forces of non-alignment, of 'positive neutralism'. A cautious anti-Americanism so far as concerned alignment with the United States was linked with a cautious approval of China, and with a distinct aversion from anything suggestive of a common front against the Peking regime.

The conference began with Nehru in command, but it ended with Chou's sharing the honours. In fact, Chou stole much of the limelight from Nehru, and worked very skilfully on the Indian prime minister's foundations to build the conference into a monument for Chinese diplomacy. Chou's speeches were admirable; his moderation was marked; his assurances were most reassuring. He aroused no suspicions, letting the current of non-alignment in Asia run its course and do his work without making obvious attempts to direct it. It was commonly assumed that he was at Bandung as the particular friend of Jawaharlal Nehru, and he did nothing to disturb the harmony which was now assumed to exist between them.

A little before this striking and, at times, theatrical conference, Chou and Nehru had jointly signed the declaration of five principles—the *Panch Sheela*—which were to have so much vogue in Asia, becoming for some years part of the diplomatic idiom of the continent. They were attached to an agreement on Tibetan trade between China and India: an agreement which, it should be noted, gave China all that it wanted but was not of any particular benefit to India. The Five Principles are a statement of good-neighbourliness between India and China; they pledge the two countries to be non-aggressive, to abstain from interference in the concerns of the other, and generally to observe an *entente cordiale* in their relations with one another. That any principles so platitudinously drafted as these are, so certain to be infringed if either side lived up to the past history of mankind, could have been taken as documents of major diplomatic consequence might seem beyond the comprehension of the sceptical observer. But the thing happened. The Five Principles distilled from the Tibetan trade agreement, and— often in slightly elaborated form—adapted for use by buddhist, muslim or other brands of Asian sentiment, were embodied in nearly all the treaties and international policy statements made by Asiatic powers in the years immediately following the Bandung Conference.

6

Peking Shows Its Strength

B Y the mid-fifties there had already begun the great
change in the attitude of China towards Russia: a
change which was to prove of crucial importance to communism's history in the second part of the twentieth century. It was determined at various turning points by the concrete decisions of individual men, and conceivably in several
instances they might have decided other than they did. The
great decisions were often made without full regard to their
effect upon Sino-Soviet relations as a whole; a mass of un-
connected decisions of government were taken in the pur-
suance of day-to-day policies in which considerations of
short-term advantage predominated. But as a whole, they
make up a picture of two governments' being forced apart
by the pressures of history, of national passion, of the
natural desire of the holders of power in a great state to
assert their sovereignty and build up their prestige.

Significantly, the leaders in both governments have
from time to time recoiled apprehensively from the edge of
the widening abyss and have made attempts at clearing the

air, at basic reconsiderations of policy, at genuine compromise. But the discussions between the governments and parties of the two countries usually ended in each side's hardening its attitudes and coming away from the conference-table convinced that the stubborn folly of the other was taking it wide-eyed towards disaster. Each of the two great communist powers felt it was its bounden duty to stand up for the interests of the communist movement as a whole; each was its brother's keeper; and thus a fervour of moral responsibility was infused into the more hard-headed motives of political rivalry.

The story is a long and complicated one, and little is to be gained by tracing it through the polemics and the recurring political crises. To date it has covered more than a decade. The first significant event in the story is the death of Stalin in 1953. China could not be expected to feel much genuine sorrow at this, for Stalin was known by the Chinese party to be a singularly faithless ally who did not hesitate to betray it, sometimes with almost casual readiness. But he was an impressive figure, a pillar of the communist cause internationally, and the focus of a mass of popular legend which seemed to most communists at the time to be indispensable to their cause. His death was therefore commemorated with as much solemnity and decorum in Peking as in Moscow. But with remarkable speed the stage was soon set for an intensive political struggle between the old and the new apostles of communism.

With Stalin's death, Mao Tse-tung was now the Number One Communist of the world. His long career had been crowned with success. A new star was in the sky. Whether or not the Russians accepted it, or even at first realised it, the man who had been their satellite had now reached a position in which, if not entitled to give world communism its marching orders, he was certainly much freer to evolve his own policies, and much less dependent on Russian assent to what he did. He had adapted his own brand of marxism to

China, but in the past the prestige of Stalin's nation and party had been so immense that he deferred formally to them in questions affecting the communist movement as a whole, and pretended that there was no essential difference between his intentions and theirs. Now he no longer felt this constraint.

This has been throughout the explaining fact in the relations of the two countries. The rift between them opened gradually. It would be interesting to know what really happened in October 1954 when Khrushchev and Bulganin visited Peking. The agreements which followed—the restoration of Port Arthur to China, the granting of long-term aid by Russia, together with Soviet help in railway construction, and the relinquishing by Russia of its share in joint stock companies in China—represented a significant effort by Moscow to promote close and cordial relations with Peking. Yet, looking back, it is possible to see that there were grave differences in 1956 at the time of the crisis in Poland and the revolution in Hungary, and throughout the various stages of the quarrel with Tito. But at the time these were veiled and their significance lost both on communism's advocates and on its interpreters in the West who were too cautious in doubting the possibility of a major rift in the 'monolithic unity of the world camp of socialism'. By 1958, however, the differences broke out openly in a dispute over foreign policy. It seems the Russians proposed during this year that they and the Chinese should operate a joint fleet in the Pacific and a jointly controlled long-range radar station on Chinese soil. The joint fleet was a remarkable idea, which may have been intended to serve the same purposes as were later envisaged in Russia's 'take-over' of Cuba. It would have drastically affected the balance of forces in the Pacific. If China had accepted the proposal, the rebuff it later suffered from Russia during the offshore islands crisis in 1959 would not have occurred. But the plan was not accepted by China. This seems to have been one of the great turning-points in post-war history.

The Chinese communists were most unwilling to leave the Kuomintang Chinese in peace. From 1958 onwards they were pressing the nationalists in Formosa, coming dangerously near to provoking a major international crisis with Chiang's protector, the United States. They asked for, and expected, Russian support. With maddening and somewhat insulting prudence, the Soviet Union, on the occasion of a visit by Khrushchev to Mao Tse-tung in 1959, made it clear to the Chinese that they could not count on Russian aid, and indicated that the Soviet government was intent on building bridges to the United States which it was quite determined should not be dynamited by Chinese adventurers.*

A little later, the shadow of the nuclear bomb fell over the relations between the two countries. China and the Bomb had become one of the dominant themes of international affairs. It seemed that China's ability to make the nuclear bomb could be a question only of time. It was held that this would transform international politics, throwing into confusion the delicate power balance in the world and vitiating the cautious approaches being made towards an accommodation between the Soviet Union and the West. It was argued that a nuclear-armed China would in some measure be able to make Russia its prisoner, dragging it along the path of Chinese ambitions and committing the senior communist state to wild adventures which, ostensibly

* Much of this sequence of events is conjectural. It should be noted that there is a contrary interpretation which puts the beginning of the quarrel as late as 1959. By this interpretation, the cause of the rift was China's dispute with India and Russia's failure to support China over the border question. According to this theory, the crisis with the United States in 1958 did not lead to worsened relations between Peking and Moscow; China got all the help it asked for from the Russians; it was not left in the lurch by Khrushchev; and called off the crisis of its own free will and out of prudence when it saw that the United States was not to be bluffed into capitulation in the confrontation over the 'offshore islands' of Quemoy and Matsu.

in the interests of world communism, would in fact be directed towards China's national interests. Or, at best, communism would be so heavily slanted by the Chinese interpretation that the Soviet Union would have to abdicate its position as the interpreter and pace-maker for communism and reconcile itself to a form of communism which would, in effect, be a Chinese and not a Russian product.

The world has awaited this event with bated breath, for its interests are as much engaged as Russia's. But a cooler judgement would shun such a catastrophic and alarmist view, arguing that mere nuclear knowledge is not sufficient for China. For the great military and political transformation to occur, which, it is predicted, will follow from China's possession of nuclear arms, it would be necessary for Chinese industry to be modernised to the point where China could actually deploy the nuclear bomb as well as possess the know-how for making it. This was, and still is, far from being the case. Nevertheless, the fact that in October 1964, the Chinese did succeed in exploding a nuclear device keeps the world on edge.

The situation would certainly have been changed if Russia had agreed to share its atomic knowledge with the Chinese People's Republic. China would have been immeasurably stronger and more to be feared, even if not ready to manufacture and stockpile nuclear weapons. But the Soviet Union was not willing to give its ally the necessary information. The Chinese have revealed that in June 1959 they asked Russia for 'a sample of an atom bomb and technical details of its manufacture'. But the Soviet government by this time had become too distrustful of China's leaders for it to respond favourably. China's rejection the year before of the Russian plan for a joint fleet had convinced Moscow that Peking was not to be considered its ally. Thenceforward the rift widened steadily. A significant event was the dismissal by the Chinese of their chief of staff, Peng Te-huai, probably because he had obstinately championed the idea of co-operation with the Soviet Union, and was willing that China should concentrate on conventional weapons, leaving to Russia the sole responsibility for the 'socialist camp's' nuclear armament. Left to devise its own military potential, pursuing its own foreign policy and made aware of Russia's unwillingness to give that policy support, China became increasingly alienated from its great coreligionist.

In the early period of the Peking regime, the Soviet Union had been of great assistance economically in furnishing technical aid to the unskilled Chinese. In the great enterprise of converting the vast land of China into a modern state, this assistance, which was very great indeed and given at a time when all of Russia's energies were needed for the internal development of the Soviet Union, was of tremendous importance. The number of Russian experts sent to China to help its economic plans is estimated as being of the order of at least fifty thousand.[1]

The removal of most of these experts during 1960 was a shattering, disintegrating blow to China. Among people so dominated by considerations of vast state planning as the Russians and Chinese, such a withdrawal of help was a deadly threat to the whole theory and practice of 'socialist planning'; as an insult it was as mortifying as its effects.

Mao Tse-tung and the communist leaders of China took a special pride in the Great Leap Forward of the Chinese economy as announced in 1958. This was a revolutionary economic policy which, by making use of new socio-economic institutions—in particular the organisation of rural areas into 'people's communes'—was intended to raise living standards in the absence of large-scale accumulations of capital and industrial resources. It was to be a short cut to communism. This grandiose plan had a particular appeal to China's leaders because it seemed to offer them the means for leading the backward parts of the world to communism, and for supplanting the Soviet Union in the primacy of world communism. It was the fulfilment of the ideas of the early 'fifties at the time of the controversy over the Chinese road to socialism and the ideas of Ranadive, the Indian communist leader. The Asians, the Latin Americans, the Africans would be lured by the Chinese example; the Russians, with their much more expensive and unimaginative form of communism—which was nothing more than state capitalism pure and simple— would be left high and dry, outmoded and outmanoeuvred.

With this grandiose project of the Great Leap Forward, the whole character of Sino-Soviet relations was changed. The Chinese had raised their sights. From thenceforward they were the competitors of Russia for primacy in the world. The path of their conflict was marked out, and anyone with a reasonably intelligent eye on the future could have foreseen the main landmarks: a worsening quarrel between the two governments; embittered relations between the two parties; the organisation of Peking as the rival Rome of the communist faith; the gradual emergence of separate and conflicting groups in the communist movement.

The Chinese cannot have been surprised that the Soviet Union showed itself extremely cool towards Peking's ambitions and, far from giving it support, instead delivered prophecies of disaster upon it. What was insupportable for the Chinese was that these prophecies came true. All the glittering expectations of the first year of the great experiment were illusory—the figures for agricultural production were appalling, the communes' boost to light industry did not materialise—and the Chinese leaders had the mortification of discovering that the facts of economics could not be changed by any amount of will or enthusiasm or 'commandism' (a marxist 'heresy' invented by them). The greatly exaggerated hopes of 1958 were paid for by three years of disastrous mismanagement and arrested industrial development. In the Chinese calendar the period 1958-61 is marked in black as 'the years of bitterness', and against this background of gloom and failure, universally recognised as an unprecedented economic crisis attributable directly to Peking's faulty policies, they had to preach to the backward areas of the world the doctrine of the invincible superiority of China's new model economy! The country's communist leadership had generated a social and economic cyclone which rocked the Chinese system, bringing down some of the parts of it in which they had taken most pride, and shaking the whole structure to its foundations.

All this time, the Chinese government was carrying on an open debate with the Russians. Primarily it was a debate with Khrushchev and the forces he represented in the CPSU. Khrushchev for the Chinese was the incarnation of revisionary marxism. His policy to them was all of a piece: a coherent repudiation, a wilful abnegation, of pure leninism which—it became clearer to them every day—was now practised in its true form only in Peking. The doctrine of peaceful coexistence; the doctrine of the uninevitability of war; the moderate attitude to the United States; the more cautious approach to the building of socialism at home—policies such as these which were reasonable enough to Soviet communists went flat against the theory and the highly radical instinct of the Chinese. China was still young in revolution; it still carried the revolutionary fire in its belly. It saw Khrushchev infected by Tito; and Titoism meant betrayal.

In pressing for a more militant policy to bring about world revolution, China has earned the obloquy of being willing to risk nuclear war. This has certainly contributed to tension with the Soviet Union. Peking has surveyed the prospect, and—in spite of reassuring statements by Chou En-lai and the fact that official utterances on the subject of nuclear war are less crudely bloodthirsty than is popularly imagined in the West—Peking is willing in the last resort to pay the price; Moscow is not. Russia will not risk its highly organised, highly centralised economy and state structure in all-out war. But China, whose organisation is much more primitive and whose people turn naturally to the village, which is less than one generation away from guerilla warfare, can probably calculate, without undue optimism, that it would survive a nuclear conflict with sufficient of its society and civilisation intact to be able to reap the benefits of victory in a war which would ruin irretrievably more advanced states. How far this line of thought predominates in official Chinese policy it is hard to say, but the belief that it does predominate leads the rest of the world to regard China as a public enemy, and seems to be driving Russia towards an understanding with the rest of the world against China.

There can be no doubt that this was the real difference between Russia and China. But the differences were often less and more subtle in regard to concrete policy than is generally supposed. For example: the impression was widespread that China was willing to challenge the West to a nuclear conflict, and that Russia cautiously preferred peace. In fact, the statements of China's leaders will be searched in vain for any indications of such outright belligerency as this impression would imply. The differences between the Soviet Union and China in this matter were less than is supposed: China was less bellicose, Russia less prudently cautious. But to pick out their views on military policy from the confusion of the texts of marxist literature, which formed the ammunition for this debate, is a wearisome and not very profitable task. Each side conned the sacred writings, and flung quotations at the other. It was a type of controversy unfamiliar in Europe since the days of the Reformation and the earlier theological disputes of the Middle Ages: a type of controversy in which it is as important to stuff the mouth of the opponent with some confuting gobbet of holy text as to take the necessary steps of negotiation to settle the question.

The countries of Asia followed this debate, but at first they were only dimly aware that their interests were affected by it. They were much more impressed by the hard facts of China's economic disaster. China's prestige tended to wane. Its military power and its diplomatic success at the Bandung Conference tended to be discounted. Formosa was still coveted by China, but as a desire which time rather than immediate action would satisfy. China, with its internal embarrassments, seemed due for a period of cautious retrenchment in external affairs.

But whatever trends there were in this direction were reversed by a renewal of China's quarrel with India and the latter's striking discomfiture.

For some time, after its success in getting control of Tibet and in the genial atmosphere generated by the Five Principles, China had been content to use India and the goodwill of Nehru for advancing its world purposes. But in the autumn of 1958, a shift in the balance of forces in the Chinese leadership brought the tougher revolutionaries to power. Events remorselessly shaped the way to conflict with India. Various factors contributed: the growing anger of the Tibetan people against their Chinese overlords; the revolt of the Khams; and the instinctive revulsion of the buddhist masses from atheistic communism. A new convulsion took place in the area where Chinese and Indian interests were fatefully interwoven. The two countries, in spite of all the efforts of Nehru to remain friendly and *Panch Sheela* notwithstanding, found themselves in overt hostility to each other. India was faced with a challenge which it could no longer ignore. The Indian government was revolutionary in origin, dedicated to national independence and the creation of a new, strong Indian nation. In the last resort, the defence of India's national interests was its main object of existence.

China completed the conquest of Tibet in 1959. It was

not willing to continue a system of loose supervision: Tibet had to be integrated with the Chinese People's Republic. As this involved blatant aggression, the act had to be gilded over as the movement of a more advanced civilisation to clean up the intolerable hell created by theocratic government and rampant feudalism. Tibet was represented by Peking as the epitome of evils produced by a reactionary regime: a system so outrageously vile as amply to justify the intervention of China. The outer world might sympathise with the Dalai Lama and with ravished Tibetan nationalism; it would, argued Peking, take a different view if it bore in mind the abuses which Tibetan nationalism covered up: China's critics pitied the plumage but forgot the dying bird.

It was of considerable importance to the Chinese government that it should succeed in this propaganda campaign because of the value to it of friendly opinion in southeast Asia. It did not want to shatter a favourable image of China by appearing to be pursuing its own brand of imperialism. But equally it was determined to swallow up Tibet.

Tibet was swallowed up. This led directly to the crucial question of the demarcation of the Indian frontier. The open conquest of Tibet brought India and China into inevitable collision. China's complete mastery of Tibet did not solve the Tibetan problem but extended it to the Sino-Indian problem. The chapter opened in 1959 is still not finished. Peking's expansionism has driven India to mobilise its resources and deploy its energies in order to set a limit to China's activities. The clash between the two countries has primarily taken the form of a dispute about the frontier between Tibet—which is now part of China—and India.*

* China's attitude to its boundaries is interesting. Historically the power of the central government reached out as far as it could, and extended in graduations of influence to the neighbouring smaller countries. China's role was that of universal monarchy: a not uncommon feature in history. But whereas in the modern world such

India, upon emancipation, had taken over the boundaries of the British Raj without the least expectation that its legal right to these might be challenged. But now the challenge came. Broadly speaking, the Chinese case was that the new Indian government had a right only to those parts of India which were unquestionably occupied by Hindus. The boundary of the British Raj, being foreign and imperialist, the Chinese argued, had been pushed forward far beyond the homeland of the Indian nation. The British had thought nothing of extending their borders a hundred miles or more beyond the true frontier of India, bringing under imperialist sway all kinds of people—predominantly mountaineers of mainly Mongol stock—in order to achieve a defensible military border. China challenged this whole concept of the Himalayan frontier. It denied that the new government in Delhi had any right in nature to the allegiance of the Himalayan people.

India declined to enter into a discussion about the ethno-geographical principles of boundaries. It based its case on past treaties and recognised frontiers. China countered this by advancing legal arguments for frontier rectification. Peking upheld that the existing boundaries between Indian and Chinese territory may very well have been fixed in the past by agreements between representatives of India and Tibet. But all such arrangements required ratification by the central government of China; this ratification had not been

---

universal empires have faded away, China still sees itself in terms of the great 'Middle Kingdom' of the past, claiming suzerainty directly or indirectly over all areas where Chinese influence has been historically asserted. Communist China has developed an obsession about reclaiming any areas which at any time in the past were accepted as Chinese-dominated. In pursuit of this, it has shown itself ready to act upon the sketchiest evidence of imperial China's relations with its neighbours. This helps to explain the traditionalist, as well as the revolutionary communist, emotions which operated on the Chinese government in its demands for rectifying the Tibetan border with India.

given. The representatives of China concerned in such negotiations, Peking contended, had not been plenipotentiaries
of the Chinese government, but emissaries whose instructions went no further than to discuss and refer proposals to
Peking for consideration. What the Indians called a 'negotiated' border had been fixed arbitrarily or by sheer fraud.
In short, the Chinese showed that they were disposed to go
over the whole line of the border with India and question
nearly every part of it.

Nehru was aggrieved when the Chinese disclosed their
hand, and complained that he had discussed the border with
Chou En-lai when he visited India in 1954. According to
Nehru, Chou had then seemed to be satisfied that the old
border should be maintained, giving the impression that
there was no border dispute at all. To this Chou En-lai replied that he had given no undertaking whatever. It would
appear that in 1954 China was not ready to engage in a
boundary dispute with India and that Chou cautiously with-
held any comment one way or the other, neither agreeing
with the Indian case nor putting forward a counter-claim.
If Nehru chose to interpret his silence as acquiescence in the
Indian claim, that, according to Chou, merely proved Nehru
an incompetent diplomatist.

Two sections of the frontier were affected in particular: the eastern section, the former North-West Frontier
Agency; and the western section, Ladakh. The eastern section was governed by the MacMahon line, named after Sir
Henry MacMahon, a senior official of the Indian government—afterwards more celebrated as the British high com-
missioner for Egypt. The line was negotiated in 1914 at a
conference in Simla, the Indian summer capital, where representatives of India, Tibet and China met. Revolution had
broken out in China and its government was very weak.
Tibet had become independent in fact and was seeking the
support of other powers for *de jure* recognition. Thus it was
not difficult for India to get Tibetan acceptance for its rather

wide border claims in return for diplomatic support for the new state of Tibet. The line was embodied in a complicated treaty which was initialled by the three countries taking part. But two days after initialling the treaty, the Chinese delegation was repudiated by Peking which objected to the treaty—but not, be it noted, on the grounds of its proposals for the Indo-Tibetan border, but because of its provisions regarding the future relations of Tibet and China, in particular the division of the former into 'outer' and 'inner' Tibet and the prohibition on the presence of Chinese troops in the outer region. In the following years, the Indian government tried to persuade China to reconsider its repudiation of the Simla treaty. Indeed, the treaty could be represented as being in China's favour since it specifically recognised China as suzerain over Tibet. But as China continued to refuse formal agreement to the treaty, the government of India eventually declared that the Simla provisions were operative between itself and Tibet. Thus was the frontier fixed on the eastern sector; but it originated from a rather questionable stroke of the diplomatic pen.

Ladakh on the western sector is a high and bleak region claimed by India to be a part of the state of Kashmir. The frontier between Kashmir and Tibet was fixed as the result of a long series of agreements. The Chinese case in challenging it was partly that the agreements were vague and partly that they had never received the assent of the central government of China. Although its claims in Ladakh had less substantial foundation than its case for a revision of the MacMahon line, China pursued them strongly and uncompromisingly. It coveted this area because it could be made to serve as a link between the Chinese province of Sinkiang and Lhasa and was perhaps essential to the retention of power over Tibet. Indeed the Chinese had already built a strategic road through Ladakh before the trouble began. The Ladakh road—through the Aksai Chin—was in fact the spark which set the dispute alight. So remote is the area, so much is it 'ten leagues beyond man's life', that the Indian government, albeit by its own claim sovereign over the district, had no intelligence from it during the year or so in which the Chinese built the road. This was held to be one of the weakest points in the Indian protest. It is generally accepted that a state must be in a position to make good its claims of frontier violation. If it does not or cannot, then it is letting its case go by default.

The frontier dispute dragged on for years, the Chinese systematically boring their way in, the Indians seeking to resolve the issue by discussion. In 1960, an Indian delegation went to Peking and laboriously sought to reason with the Chinese on the basis of treaties and maps. The Indian negotiators rather ingenuously felt that if they could state their case convincingly, the Chinese must accept it and own themselves in the wrong. They do not seem to have realised that the Chinese were simple using argument as an adjunct to force. Having determined on a border revision, the facts of the case were regarded by them merely as a decent veneer of reason for a policy they were resolved to implement come what may.

Why China was so bent on revising its frontiers at the cost of a breach with India still remains obscure. The territory claimed, even allowing for the strategic usefulness of Ladakh to the Chinese presence in Tibet, was not so valuable as to appear worth arousing India's enmity to get it. Compared with the vast land mass of China and its other dependent territories, it was of small importance. The resort to force in order to get it threw to the winds India's friendship which had been offered to China gratuitously. It was to damage the standing of communism in the eyes of the Indian people, thereby imperilling whatever chances had existed for the Indian Communist Party. And it was to go diametrically against the policy of Russia which was seeking to create for itself in the eyes of the Indians and indeed of all Asian peoples the image of a truly benevolent great power which sought to benefit India, asking nothing in return save that India should not align itself with the western camp. Why did China over-ride such considerations?

Perhaps China was simply old-fashioned. Its diplomacy is tenacious: what China has once held it is exceedingly unwilling to let go. It claims that all the land under Chinese sway at the height of the power of the Manchu emperors is still rightfully Chinese. The passage of time and the vicissitudes of systems make no difference: what has been Chinese must be Chinese again. In this, the new revolutionary government in Peking is displaying naked imperialism and power politics. The idea of communism's fulfilling a destiny in restoring the boundaries of the Chinese empire— by the conquest of Tibet and the rectification of the frontier with India—weighs very deeply with the leaders of the party. It seems to touch something deep within the Chinese spirit and is therefore endorsed by Chinese public opinion. So it may be that some great compulsion of national mood was responsible for China's outward thrust against India.

But other less emotive reasons played their part and these are rather more susceptible to reasoned analysis. For all its 'Bandung era' politeness towards India as an Asian country, China was determinedly opposed to Delhi's intention of being a comparable influence to Peking in Asia. It was obnoxious to China that India should claim to have devised a successful non-communist model for Asian statehood, one which other non-communist countries in the continent could follow in their search for independence and modernisation. India's democracy, the much advertised success of its economic planning, its liberal institutions such as the independent judiciary and the free press—all this was a challenge to Peking. The challenge was aggravated by the reputation and strength of the Indian army. The armed forces of the new India were inherited from the British; wreathed with the laurels of past prowess, their prestige served to enhance India's authority far beyond its borders and to make India's weight felt in areas of south-east Asia which China looked on as territories destined for its own expansion. Peking resented the strength of India's military reputation because it had a suspicion that the Indian army's power was grossly overestimated, and that if it were put to the test of a fight with its own disciplined Red Army, Nehru's army would buckle and collapse. The Indian army played the same role as 'the fleet in being' in European strategic theory of the nineteenth century, and the Chinese were intent on dethroning it.

There was also Russia. The Soviet Union's intimate relations with India were a standing grievance with China. Peking saw with growing indignation the millions of rubles made available to India: money which could have given the much needed impetus for building up China's communist economy. China's leaders seethed with fury at the effect on India's prestige in Asia of Russia's friendship. They may have felt that a shrewd blow at India, whatever temporary obloquy it occasioned, would both shatter that prestige, so unnatural and so undeserved, thereby leaving China alone in the field, and also remove India as an impertinent competitor for Russia's political and economic support.

Another factor may also have been operative: China was contemptuous of India. It held that India was an imitation of a European country in the East, so much influenced, indeed conditioned, during its long subjection to Britain that it had lost its Asian soul and become westernised. China's leaders were convinced that by this apostasy India's government could not be given credence in Asian affairs. Admittedly, they said, the bulk of the Indian people was still unaffected and had an Asian soul. India was reclaimable; but this could only come about through revolution and the casting off of the westernised upper class which held the power of the newly independent nation firmly in its grasp. The Chinese, it must be said, were hardly in a position validly to make this sneering judgement for China itself, in going communist, had taken over from the West a complete apparatus of society and had repudiated the institutions of China's past. But doubtless they felt that communist employment of western methods was less 'debilitating' and un-Asian.

These calculations and considerations caused China to strike out at India in the autumn of 1962. It was not a full-scale war, but it had the effects of one. It was not the confrontation of the total mobilised strength of China against that of India, but it had many of the consequences which this would have brought about. The Indian army had only three divisions engaged, but such was their humiliation that the prestige of the army as a whole suffered severely. It was a rout in remote mountain country, a lost engagement, but it carried with it almost the consequences of a lost war. From these dismal months of the frontier war came a sharp downward lurch of India's prestige in Asia.

It is true that China did not secure an acknowledgement from India that it had been worsted. By diplomacy, India avoided negotiation and thus thwarted the Chinese leaders' ambition for a dictated settlement as the concomitant of military defeat. But of India's claim to be a model for Asia and the equal of China there was hardly a scrap left. India had been forced to abandon, in practice if not explicitly, its theory of non-alignment—the theory which had been the essence of its claim to leadership in Asia and the world—and, driven to take refuge under the shelter of American and British power, had confessed the inadequacy of its arms and diplomacy to defend itself. As is not infrequently the case in international politics, China's shameful act of aggression was offset by an increase of prestige for the victor—and a deeper respect for its brightening prospects in the world.

In planning the operation, China had clearly placed hope in the activity and influence of the communist party in

India. Indeed, there is evidence that in Peking there was the same besotted overvaluation of communism in India as used to mark the Russian fixed belief in communism in England during the benighted years of misinformation under Stalin. It may be that China merely mistimed its confidence. With the death of Nehru, communism may well grow rapidly to become a major power in the country. With good reason, China may expect it to put a hobble in India's resistance to the plans of Chinese communism. But in 1962, the result of China's actions was not to make of communism a strong force in India but to split the Indian Communist Party. It divided into three groups: one siding with China, one with Russia, while the third—vividly aware of the harm communism in India had previously done itself by appearing to be identified at various times in the past with antinational forces—offered support in a dramatic way to the embattled government of India. This division was to become important to China as it developed its bid for the support of communism throughout the world in its clash with the Soviet Union.

Both before and after the border war, the Chinese worked with great skill to isolate India from states on its borders. One by one Peking offered to negotiate agreements over the frontiers of these countries with China. It was prepared to go to considerable lengths to ensure that they did not make common cause with India. Thus it has come about that Afghanistan, Pakistan, Nepal and Burma have all engaged in friendly negotiations with China. In this way, India has been robbed of the sympathy of its neighbours. Having found China so accommodating, they have been easily susceptible to the Peking-inspired inference that India is being unnecessarily awkward and truculent. The border with Burma was fixed in 1961, that with Pakistan (involving the surrender by China of no more than 2,000 square miles of barren territory) in 1963, and an agreement with

Afghanistan is to be expected. Some of these agreements may verge onto something very close to an alliance, for India has been conspicuously lacking in the knack of winning the friendship of smaller neighbours. In particular, it has obstinately brawled with Pakistan, and so far, even now when China's aggressive intentions have become clear, the government still is reluctant to come to an accommodation with Pakistan, and seems to prefer the dangers inherent in Indo-Pakistani hostility to a settlement on Kashmir. The damaging consequences to India of an unfriendly Pakistan are a legacy of Nehru's policy. The 'success' of Nehru's foreign policy is one of the great myths of our time.

7

The New Apostle of Communism

W HAT to do about China became an increasing pre-occupation for Russia. Communism in China had passed from Russian control and was now, indeed, attempting to control Russia. The irony was that China remained relatively weak. Though its army was huge and with a high morale, especially after its worsting of India, China had a poor economic infrastructure for large-scale war. However, the Chinese had other soucres of strength in their situation, and were ready to carry on political warfare with confidence and boldness.

The frontier war with India certainly did not lead to any improvement in China's relations with Russia. Quite the reverse; they deteriorated even further because Russia, throughout the Sino-Indian dispute—with only one notable lapse—gave material aid and comfort to India. This rankled deeply with China.

At the same time there were rumbles of a more fundamental conflict which threatened to place China and Russia in deadly enmity with one another: an enmity which may last indefinitely and be one of the principal factors of history. It concerns the Sino-Russian frontier: a matter much graver than the border dispute between India and China. The frontier as it exists at present took shape as the result of continuous pressure on China during two-and-a-half centuries by an expansionist Russia. Though China had acquiesced by treaty to all but a few undemarcated sections of the frontier, it regarded large tracts of territory, which were undeniably Russia's, as having been filched from China by imperialist manoeuvres. It felt itself the victim of 'unequal treaties', not only in regard to European powers in the nineteenth century, but also in regard to tsarist Russia. Moreover, whereas the unequal treaties with the West have now been abrogated or rectified, those with Russia are still extant. China dwells on the fact that large spaces in central Asia and in Siberia, which are essentially Asian in geography, ethnic character, culture and tradition, have been arbitrarily occupied by Russia, which has then sought to settle them with an immigrant population. This effort has been only partly successful, and the lands in which China claims interest are still to a large degree underinhabited. This is an important fact in the thinking of the regime in Peking which is becoming increasingly anxious to siphon off China's excessive population.

Its leaders have sought to open up discussion of frontier rectification by pressing for a settlement of the undemarcated areas, which are mainly in Sinkiang. But they leave little doubt that behind this particular issue there looms a much larger question: a challenge to Russia on the basis of equity and history of its right to continue occupying this Asian soil. China's support of 'Asia for the Asians' is never far below the surface in its sparring with Russia.

Peking has interests in Outer Mongolia which also threaten its relations with Moscow. The story in Outer Mongolia has followed the same lines as in the rest of the territory overlapping the Sino-Russian frontier. Russia has exerted a separatist pull, and so successfully that in 1947 Outer Mongolia was recognised as a sovereign state, detached from China. Formally it is independent, and therefore not directly annexed by the Soviet Union. But Russian protection, Russian economic interests and Russian control of the Mongolian Communist Party, are still effective. Peking has never assented in its heart to this arrangement, and has sought ever since, though so far with conspicuous lack of success, to reassert its influence and to limit Russia's.

By the end of 1963 the breach between Moscow and Peking was widening despite attempts to come to terms. Their quarrel and its development are plain to see in the speeches, articles and statements of both sides, and in the exchange of letters between the communist parties.* In 1963, the Russians somewhat reluctantly agreed to what was intended as a supreme effort by the theoreticians of both parties at the highest level to analyse their differences and work out a reconciliation. But when the Chinese delegation arrived in Moscow for the conference in the July of that year, they found the Russians much more interested in negotiations with the West for ending the testing of nuclear bombs than in coming to an accommodation with Peking. Proclaiming that they were prepared to wait for the questions at issue to be resolved, the Chinese withdrew from the profitless and damaging wrangle.

Russia went on to sign, in August 1963, the 'partial' test-ban agreement with America and Britain. China was not a party to this and made it clear that it disapproved of it. For China the test-ban treaty was clear evidence that Russia had become closely aligned with the West. In Peking's book, a nation was either on one side or on the other in this great issue of the age. Russia had chosen: it was

---

* A clear path may be traced through the bewildering jungle of polemics and vilification by the aid of the catalogue of documents included in David Floyd's indispensable book, *Mao against Khrushchev*. (See Reading List.)

in the camp of those who sought to maintain the status quo. China was in the opposite camp.

There were more ideological disputes, more threats and menaces. Finally Khrushchev announced that the Soviet party would summon a meeting in Moscow of all the communist parties of the world, to begin on December 14, 1964. This meeting, it is clear, was intended by him to prepare the ground for China's exclusion from the common life of communism.

The quarrel, which had arisen for valid political and ideological reasons, began more and more to display the characteristics of a racial feud. Russians and Chinese had at heart a profound mistrust of each other. They were antagonistic races. The Chinese could not forget that Russia, before the days of communism, had always seemed China's arch-enemy; the Russian armies, poised in the north and west for a descent on China, have inherited in the Chinese mind the place of the nomad peoples beyond the Great Wall. For Russia, China meant the unnumbered hordes which could sweep them from their thinly populated empire in Siberia and Central Asia. Thus the sophisticated ideological dispute was beginning to turn into a primitive racial hostility, beyond the skill of the statesmen to overcome.

The rest of the world concluded that the two great communist parties were being inexorably forced apart. Henceforward it seemed that there were to be two Romes in the communist communion, and that, if not in actual conflict, they would certainly be in active competition with one another.

Then, in October 1964, Khrushchev fell. His going astonished the world. One day he appeared at the height of his power; no word was heard of any difficulties in his position; the next day he was gone. The world was left to puzzle over the workings of the complex political system which had, out of the blue, produced this mighty overthrow.

The Chinese leaders had identified Khrushchev with everything in the Russian attitude which had brought Moscow and Peking into collision, and they did not mince their words in condemning him. Though it is difficult to estimate the direct influence of the Chinese Communist Party within the Soviet Union, Peking's position was helped by the fact that, though the Chinese were deeply unpopular and there was wide support among the Russian people for Khrushchev's policy, there was an influential section within the Soviet party which was deeply disturbed at the way in which Khrushchev was steering the dispute. The former alliance with China was being turned into actual hostility, and all the solid advantages which could come from good relations between these two great states were being lost. Khrushchev's manner, his irascibility, bluntness and volatile susceptibilities crippled any possibility of handling the delicate relationship between China and Russia with prudence and statesmanship. China might be very unreasonable, might need closest watching. Yet, to critics of his policy, Khrushchev's strong animosity against China was pushing Moscow towards a policy which ran counter to its interests and more in keeping with those of the United States than of the Soviet Union. Khrushchev had to be removed if the bias in Soviet policy was to be corrected.

Even so, his fall did not mean a complete reversal of his policy. Russia's aim was still to keep China 'in its place' —but by following more subtle and circumspect methods, taking the heat out of the dispute, and avoiding the situation created by Khrushchev, in which Moscow seemed to be suicidally abandoning Russia's own interests and those of world communism.

China had appealed to communists outside Russia. It had had some overt success in appealing to communist parties in the West as well as in the East, where its ascendancy was in general unquestioned. Lively pro-Chinese groups developed in the Belgian, French and Italian parties, and also, it seems, in the British. These were amazed at the ultra-flexibility of Russian policy in recent years, and shocked at the extent to which Khrushchev was influenced by personal feelings. At the same time, many communists who did not adhere to the Peking line grew alarmed at the way things were going; to them the Chinese, though tiresome and difficult, did not seem so diabolical. They began to expostulate. The Rumanian prime minister tried to mediate. Togliatti, the leader of the Italian Communist Party, went to Russia to try to convince Khrushchev of the folly of driving China to extremes and to dissuade him from forcing on communists throughout the world the agonising issue of China's expulsion from the socialist camp. Togliatti died in the Soviet Union in the summer of 1964 without having been able to get Khrushchev to meet him. But before his death he wrote a long memorandum on the problems confronting the communist world; this, his political testament, was published and undoubtedly had great influence.

China's appeal to the public opinion of the communist world thus bore fruit. The view gained ground in communist circles that personal factors were being allowed to distort the course of communist policy. This opinion coincided with the views of many cautious party men in Russia and, conjoined with internal political factors, helped to seal Khrushchev's doom.

His fall was thus a gain for the Chinese. But it was a limited gain. Whatever the influence of the Sino-Soviet dispute on the course of events in Moscow, Khrushchev's fall did not mean that Moscow was capitulating to Peking. Russia would continue to pursue its own way. Even so, it would be likely to be more careful about incurring Chinese enmity. For one thing, China's explosion of a nuclear bomb in the very week of Khrushchev's fall in October 1964 made it a much more formidable figure in the world. The general lines of Russian policy under Khrushchev would be maintained, but there would be a more prudent approach to achieving its basic objectives. The Soviet leaders would abstain from Khrushchev's rash practice, all too congenial to Russian national opinion, of goading China by rebukes and jibes in public utterances. They had gained a new insight into what Chinese hostility could mean, and henceforward would try to placate China and not recklessly drive it to extremes.

In the months and years ahead, the Soviet Union may perhaps renew a measure of economic aid to China; its technicians may again operate there; cultural and goodwill missions may again be exchanged; and there may be an end to sniping by party theoreticians. But on the great question of the Bomb, Russia will prove as uncooperative as before. China is most unlikely to get any Russian help in fitting teeth to its nuclear device; and without such help several years of hard research are still ahead for China. Only in the unlikely event—which would be in flat contradiction to all observable trends in Soviet society—of a resurgence of stalinism would there be a real change in Russian policy. And even if the country were to get a government determined to be more pugnacious towards the West, it is probable that this would not take any more compliant a line towards China.

Still, with Khrushchev removed, Peking is not likely to ask for too much. Khrushchev was the supreme foe, and Chinese resentment became concentrated on him. Fundamentally, China has never desired to quarrel with Russia; the latter has been the pace-setter in the dispute. Moreover China is itself in a transitional stage. Chinese communism is approaching an age-crisis; its leaders are nearly all old men, and they must shortly pass from the scene. There is a serious gap between them and the generation which will succeed them. Mao is as much exalted as Stalin ever was, and China will pay the price for its own personality cult. What will happen when Mao goes is unpredictable, but an upheaval of some kind is highly probable. So for this reason alone there are uncertainties about the future relationship between China and Russia.

Previous experience would suggest that where China is conscious of its weakness, it is, in action, if not in words or theory, exceedingly prudent, walking delicately like Agag. It conducted its Korean adventure without getting itself involved in a bigger war than it had bargained for. And the most dangerous threat to world peace since 1945 —the Cuban crisis of 1962—was provoked, not by China, for all its talk of 'imperialist paper tigers' and revolutionary struggle, but by Russia, by the 'responsible' Khrushchev.

But for all the uncertainties, one thing seems clear: China is likely to press on with its activities directed to the under-developed countries of the world. It is impelled by a sense of mission. Chinese communism is, perhaps unconsciously, reverting to the old universalism of Chinese culture. This had assumed that the Chinese way of life, Chinese institutions and methods—all things Chinese—were a boon and a blessing to all the lesser peoples surrounding China, and that it was its mission to spread them over a deprived and grateful world. As the Hans had sinified large tracts of Asia, so the Chinese communists look to the sinification of Asia, Africa and Latin America: sinification in the modern context meaning the adoption of the Chinese version of communism. This they regard as being peculiarly suited, in a way that Russia's 'European' brand of communism is not, to the needs and circumstances of poor, backward countries.

In seeking to extend the revolution, Peking has always paid great attention to land reform. Wherever there are acute agrarian problems, China's communist leaders see an opportunity for agitation. Indeed, the movement for land reform has been a chief motive of Chinese communism. After all, this has been its history in China itself, and communism in other countries has derived its heat and fury from the land-hungry peasantry. Peking does not feel it necessary to dwell on its ultimate solution of the agrarian problems of the peasantry after communism comes to power: the evolution of land reform into collectivisation and communes. It is taking the line that one step is enough for the time being, and that the immediate step is to give the peasant land.

During its conflict with Russia, China has sought to become a decisive influence in determining the communist party line all over the world. But it is the underdeveloped countries the Chinese desire to capture, and it is here where their success would be most significant. Because of their aggressive policy over the Indian frontier, they cannot hope to be very popular in India; yet it speaks much for the emotional appeal of China's brand of communism that the Indian party continues to be divided between pro-Russian and pro-Chinese wings. In the communist states of eastern Europe, the Chinese have been worsted by the Russians; yet they have managed to capture the allegiance of Albania. The task of swinging over established communist regimes is, however, so great and the organised strength of the Soviet party so dominant, that the Chinese may despair of converting communism as a whole to their interpretation of it, and be content that the international movement should bifurcate, leaving them in unchallengeable dominance over one half of it.

The failure of the Great Leap Forward of 1958 is now regarded as of little significance both by the Chinese themselves and by the outside world. The failure's damaging effects to China's prestige have worn off and China is now riding high in the admiration or fear of the outside world. The Chinese are satisfied in their own minds that they have discovered *the* way; and if there have been mishaps in following it, they take comfort from the old slogan of communism: 'One step backward, two steps forward'. Chou En-lai, in a celebrated tour of Africa at the end of 1963 and the beginning of 1964, pronounced the African situation very promising for revolution. The Chinese communists are willing to take their time, to retreat in the certainty that they will advance again. They are convinced that they are co-operating with history. They regard themselves, with some reason, as being today more creative intellectually than the Russian communists, and they think especially that it is to their advantage that the world is moving towards an upheaval of the poorer masses of humanity. They offer the more primitive communism: a communism which is relatively easy to operate and which caters for the passions and pristine hates of all the most drab and tormented parts of human society. As Russia was formerly, so now China is attracted to all the regions that are regarded as calamitous and deprived; out of these they aim to fashion a society which, though not utopian, is governed according to a rough puritanical code of sharing poverty equally. The Russians have now their part with the 'haves'. Their philosophy is tainted by revisionism. This may make Russian communism more acceptable to the advanced economic societies of the world, but it thereby becomes less acceptable to the primitive societies. The Chinese, strengthened by such arguments, are convinced that no community which is really backward would ever choose Russia as the guide to revolution.

Chinese universities are giving scholarships to young people from Africa and Latin America. Many of these appear content to be indoctrinated, and will return to their own countries confident that they have seen the new light in the East, and willing to be the disciples of the new eastern apostle of communism. All this while, China itself is being organised to make it fit the role of the arch-evangelist of communism. Its diplomatists have been learning the facts of international life, but have not been conditioned by this experience into a willingness to compromise with the enemy. Its generals have helped to spread the prestige of

China everywhere. Mao Tse-tung has been increasingly presented by Chinese propaganda as one of the major communist prophets: the continuator and equal of Marx, Engels, Lenin and Stalin.

The difference between the world of yesterday and the world of today is that Peking has replaced Moscow as the potent source of subversion. As world forces, in general uncontrollable, mark out different areas for crisis and convulsion, revolutionaries in such areas will look to China for guidance. Russia will try to compete, but its voice will almost certainly count for less than China's.

It is with such world-wide interests that China's policy now has to do. Its strategy takes in at least three continents. But in the heady enthusiasm for revolutionary tactics in Cuba and Zanzibar, and for *realpolitik* ventures in Albania, Peking does not overlook its immediate task, its unfinished business in Asia: the removal of American influence. It is probably less set on bringing the smaller states of Asia under direct communist control, though it strongly supports their communist parties, than on barring American influence in them. Vietnam, Formosa, the Philippines, Indonesia, Thailand—all attract attention of this sort from China. Even Japan, though a power of quite a different order from these, is grouped in the same category. Whatever the complexion of its government, Japan is a great danger to Peking as long as it constitutes a centre of American influence in Asia.

All these countries fear for their independence, and are naturally afraid of China. This gives them a strong inclination towards the United States. Their nationalism can find support in America. But their nationalism can also be flattered and cosseted by China. Communism is at least as skilful as American propaganda in offering the nationalists of small countries the flattering regard for which they hanker, and may also seem to offer guarantees of their independence as assuring as America's. Moreover, in nearly all of them the dominant trend of public opinion is in favour of what may vaguely be termed socialism. People in these countries may have little concept of what socialism really is, but there is a widespread feeling that the world has moved into a socialist phase, and that it behoves them to move with the times. This mood inclines them to look with a more favourable eye on communism than on American capitalism. Communism is able to appeal to the myth of Asianism—of Asia for the Asians. This still seems to be the guiding principle of many Asian nationalists, and it makes them fear alliance with any western power. They are so liable to be gulled by this that it is an easy task for a diplomacy as longsighted and wily as Chou En-lai's to turn them against their ultimate defender—the United States—to engage them in strife with other countries in south-east Asia, and eventually to entrap them into subjection to China. Peking's way now seems smooth. It has only to follow the principles of judo. It must not exert brute strength of itself, but push the states of Asia this way and that, using the energies they are themselves generating to move them in a particular direction, and then by increasing the pressure to despatch them in one throw.

America has sought to shepherd the smaller fringe countries into defence groupings. Two such alliances exist, one in south-east Asia (SEATO), and the other further to the west (CENTO). The peculiarity of both these organisations is that their military strength derives not from their members *in situ*, but from the western powers with which they are connected. The smaller countries purchase what they deem to be protection by affording the western powers bases and footholds for possible operations in the regions concerned.*

These have been rather inert and sleepy alliances. That

---

* Actually, the SEATO treaty does not commit the signatories automatically to full military action in the event of aggression against one of their number. It binds them only to consultation, though clearly it was the hope of the framers of the treaty that this con-

they were doubtfully conceived is shown by the fact that many of the countries eligible to become pact members decided to opt out. In south-east Asia, only Thailand and the Philippines became members. Indonesia and Malaya remained aloof. It was not because these countries favoured China or were indifferent to the risk of passing under Chinese control; but they had doubts about SEATO's effectiveness, were as unwilling to surrender sovereignty to the United States as to China, and judged it prudent not to infuriate Peking by being used too evidently as pawns in western manoeuvres.

The way the Chinese overcome such American-inspired alliances is shown in its most characteristic form in Vietnam. Vietnam was partitioned in 1954 according to the terms of the Geneva Agreement which concluded the war in Indochina between the French and the Viet Minh. The northern half of the country is communist. Its government has attempted to enlarge its sphere of freedom from the Chinese, skilfully balancing itself between Russia and China. But in the upshot it is a tool at the disposal of the Chinese.

The president of the Democratic Republic of North Vietnam, Ho Chi Minh, is a typical figure of oriental communism. He is the organiser par excellence; he is the conspirator, the manager of the Vietnamese Communist Party, the politician who uses the party with great and deadly effect. Nobody should under-rate him; he has been for many years the master of a solid basis of power and is the most considerable figure among communists of south-east Asia. Yet he should not be over-rated. The Chinese communists, while respecting Ho, refuse, rightly, to allow him to be compared with Mao Tse-tung. It may seem to some a curious

sultation would lead to common action. An important aspect of the alliance is the provision for various forms of continuing activity, amongst which is included police action against communist subversion in the region.

piece of communist snobbery that so much store should be set by dogmatic writing; but given that this is so, Ho's standing in the movement is substantially lower than Mao's. Mao's prestige derives not only from his being the leader of so powerful a party and state but also from his status as a political thinker: a status which, in Chinese eyes, entitles his writings to be added to the sacred canon of marxism-leninism. Their claim for Mao may be exaggerated, and in fact his principal contribution to communist doctrine is less a theoretical than a historical view of the contradictions which operate in society: contradictions which, according to Mao, are as much likely to appear in a communist state as in one which has yet to experience 'socialist revolution'. But even if, to the objective student of communism, Mao's contribution is less spectacular than the Chinese claim, it cannot be doubted that his writings are voluminous, pungent, wide-ranging and influential. All that Ho has produced is one small pamphlet on colonialism in which he sought to prove that the stalinist analysis was valid for French Indo-china.* Ho is emphatically the man of action, not the creative thinker. He operates on lines set out by other people. He has not produced a scheme of thought which enables him to operate by his own direction. To this extent, though greatly admired for his revolutionary achievements, he is held in much less esteem than Mao by the Chinese communists and their adherents in Asia.

The southern half of Vietnam is under a government which, in spite of friction in its relations with the United States, looks to America for patronage and protection. For a period after 1954, it seemed as if a system of coexistence

---

* Le procès de la colonisation française, Paris 1926. Bernard B. Fall, in The Two Viet-Nams (see Reading List), describes it as a 'slapdash, naïve pamphlet' (p. 86). Apart from this, the sum total of Ho's writing, according to Fall, consists of collections of speeches, a small volume of verse written while in a Chinese prison, and a play, Le dragon de bambou, which failed when produced in Paris in 1923.

had been reached between South and North Vietnam, but since 1962 the North has undertaken a systematic guerilla assault upon the South which is designed to bottle up the Vietnamese Republic's administration in the towns, gain control of the country districts and gradually erode the government's effectiveness and popular support. At the time of writing, this attack is developing very favourably for the communists.

What then of SEATO? By the terms of the Geneva Agreement which partitioned Vietnam, South Vietnam was specifically barred from joining SEATO. So that, albeit all the members of the alliance are agreed that one of its principal objects is the defence of new states, SEATO to all intents and purposes has been powerless to come to the help of South Vietnam as the structure of the new state crumbles under the forces of subversion.*

The United States builds alliances: China, by diplomacy and threats, demolishes them. China promotes guerila warfare by inciting and supporting other people to take arms against non-communist, pro-western governments. This

* In its operations against South Vietnam, China has been helped by the ambitions and susceptibilities of Prince Sihanouk, the ruler of the neighbouring country of Cambodia. Peking's handling of Sihanouk is a classic example of its skill in getting unlikely instruments to serve its purposes. Sihanouk will clearly cease to count for anything if communist power ever becomes supreme in south-east Asia; but he has convinced himself that communist power is waxing and America's waning, and that therefore he must get himself in China's good books. Accordingly he is very attentive to the bait dangled on the communist hook; he will take what communism has to offer, even though it is a short-term offer. At the same time he seeks a double guard for his interests, just in case, by negotiating with the Americans. But he feels that the United States is most likely to be of benefit to him if he arouses its concern by turning towards China. In 1964, he has complicated the position in South Vietnam very considerably by allowing guerila forces from the North to pass through Cambodia to operate on the western flank of the South.

gives the United States an intractable problem to grapple with. It finds it difficult to identify the enemy to be directly dealt with. Its policies and positions are the target of a coherent plan, but the shots come from the dark. America is hindered by the lack of a visible, tangible adversary to shoot back at. It is a long tussle and the end is not yet. China maintains constant pressure against American bases in south-east Asia, and is at work all the time in trying to incite country after country to insist on the abolition of the American presence in their midst. Peking carries on a persistent, eroding propaganda which aims at persuading the world that it is the United States which is the trouble-maker. All this is linked with China's inflexible determination to overthrow Chiang Kai-shek's regime on Formosa and to drive the American Seventh Fleet from the Far East.

Lying between America's Asian alliances and Australasia is the largest of the countries of south-east Asia, Indonesia. With a hundred million inhabitants it is the fifth largest state in the world. Its ruler, Sukarno, is an opportunist nationalist somewhat of the Mussolini type, and he finds in the situation in south-east Asia a climate congenial to the nurturing of his ambitions. He confronts one neighbour and then another. He confronted the Dutch and by persistence gained West Irian (formerly Dutch New Guinea); he now confronts Malaysia and hopes to gain all Borneo. Peking has only to encourage him and wait. Sukarno's expansionist urge is likely to provoke a war with some neighbouring state. The Chinese may hope to do much through an understanding with the Indonesian Communist Party, one of the largest and best organised communist parties in Asia. It will have its chance in the confusion of war; it may bring all Indonesia firmly into the Chinese camp, and thereby enormously strengthen China's efforts to push the United States out of south-east Asia.

So far, America has refused to be dislodged, but its foothold becomes ever more precarious. The fringe areas, where Chinese power is thrusting forward and the United States is counter-thrusting, are kept at fever pitch; little happens there which is not due to the operation, direct or indirect, of China and the United States. The agitation and self-immolation of buddhists in South Vietnam; the military revolutions in Saigon; the confrontation of Indonesia against Malaysia; the unrest in Burma—all these, at least in the manner of their working out, can be traced directly to the struggle of China to rid Asia of American power and influence.

Throughout its long duel with the United States, China has undoubtedly been hampered by the American-inspired policy of non-recognition of the Chinese People's Republic and by America's successful efforts to keep it out of the United Nations. But the United States cannot succeed indefinitely in this policy: sooner or later other countries will demur to the point of abandoning it and of defying the constraints which the United States puts on them to observe it. The doctrine of non-recognition and its deployment as an instrument of policy, is an American invention. Normal practice in international relations is to recognise the facts of power for what they are. It is probable that the French decision to recognise Mao's regime is the first step on the way which will lead the Chinese People's Republic into the United Nations. General de Gaulle's policy is a marked innovation, but is not inconsistent with his political character. His habitual tendency is to think of foreign politics in terms of power-centres and of the reactions of power-holders in any given part of the world. He is to a great degree indifferent to ideology. The government of Mao Tse-tung, he holds, is acting in much the same way and for the same basic interests as the government of Chiang Kai-shek would act, were that strong and in power on the mainland of China. By this analysis, the ideological considerations which the United States invokes to justify its strenuous boycott of the

Chinese People's Republic appear to be of little consequence to de Gaulle.

China may aim at thwarting the United States by forming a bloc of states which desire to be neutral and uncommitted in the great power struggle. By this means, strange associations may cut across the existing orientations of countries. Out of the instability of international relations comes one of the great opportunities for China.

When China eventually achieves membership of the United Nations, it will be interesting to see how its relations with Russia develop in the Security Council. Those who see advantage for themselves in the conflict between the two great communist states may well think it good policy to support China's admission. It will place a new strain on relations within the communist camp. China and Russia may find themselves repeatedly voting in opposite lobbies, though on matters in which their essential national interests are not engaged they will certainly try to maintain harmony. But they will be well aware of the satisfaction their differences will give in quarters hostile to communism, and considerations of mere prudence will constrain them to restrict the occasions for these differences. Moreover, China's membership of the United Nations will increase rather than decrease its effectiveness as a revolutionary power, and Peking is likely to lay claim to a full part in all UN activities.

Every year, the number of China's embassies and consulates will increase. Peking will wheel into position its agents of propaganda, subversion and political intelligence. Hitherto China has waged a belligerent world-wide diplomacy in conditions which have, by and large, been unfavourable. They are not likely to remain so for long if China acts prudently as well as ambitiously.

This is perhaps the crucial factor. China has shown that it can be forceful and adventurous: can it also act with sense and sensibility? So far, in cultivating Africans and the people of Latin America, Peking has put over its theoretical case with much éclat and wedged a substantial foot in the door in these areas; but it has failed to appreciate that it has undone much of its work by acting with a high-handedness and superiority—probably the effect of the tremendous disdain the Chinese have traditionally shown towards the outside world—which Africans and Latin Americans interpret as racialism and overweening pride. So the alliance which is developing between these peoples and China is definitely ambiguous. It is cemented by a feeling that their interests merge; but it is conditioned by a deep suspicion, by the nagging thought that they are unlikely to be united by genuine sympathy or affection, and that they need a long spoon in supping with one another.

But how long is a long spoon? China's relations with 'the third world' are not likely to be confined to diplomatic contacts. At the time of writing* it has become clear that China is interested in exerting direct influence by means of military 'assistance' to African countries. Chinese arms and advisers are reported in Somalia and have made their presence felt in the conflict in the Congo between central government and rebel forces.

Even more significant may be the decision of President Julius Nyerere of the United Republic of Tanganyika and Zanzibar to accept a Chinese military mission to help train his army. Although Nyerere seems to intend a 'balanced plan' in which several major powers will join, opening the door to Chinese military personnel is likely to give Peking an influence quite disproportionate to the size of its mission of eleven army instructors. The Chinese communists have a very real appreciation of the value of military contacts, and may hope to obtain something like the ubiquitous and sinister influence which their penetration of the Whampoa Military Academy gave them in China. The prospects of what could happen in Africa as a result of Chinese military missions there are certainly daunting.

* Autumn 1964.

Conclusion

THE history of communism is fascinating because it is the study of persevering efforts, by a disciplined body of men of extraordinary resilience, to obtain the monopoly of power. They are the servants of communist dogma, and in their private talk and their public statements they continually resort to dogma to explain and justify their acts and intentions. Yet in fact, as experience has shown, they have been obliged by circumstances to wear their dogma lightly.

There have been significant differences in the history of communism in the two continents. In Europe, communism began as a protest gainst poverty. But in Asia—where poverty is much greater than it was in Europe—communism has proved attractive as a means of establishing a new basis of government where the old traditional bases have been discredited and made of no account by the ideas of the age. This difference explains some of communism's recent history.

In China, particular circumstances and events have intervened to shape the course which the Chinese communist party and government have taken. In theory—according to received dogma—this course should not diverge significantly from the trail blazed by the Soviet Union. The aims and philosophy of Chinese communism continue to be the same as those of Russian communism. In theory, both are part of the international communist movement, of the 'united socialist camp'. But, in fact, Peking has set itself up as communism's new eastern capital from which illumination, action and command are to radiate over Asia (and indeed the whole world if circumstances allow).

For reasons of its quarrel with Russia, China has set itself the task of preserving leninism in all its purity, and of using leninism for its prime appeal to backward countries so as to organise them for world revolution.

If, in some other part of the world which is traditionally a directing centre of humanity (or develops into such), a similar body of men, actuated by the ideas of communism, should come to power, then these also, following the imperatives of the search for and enlargement of power, are likely to find dogma of increasing irrelevance under the pressure of circumstances. In the course of time they will be likely to drift apart from their fellows in Moscow and Peking, and to operate a communism coloured by the events and needs of their part of the world rather than by the dogmatic precepts of 'orthodox' communism. But for this, it would be necessary for them to achieve power in some part of the world which is 'metropolitan', not 'provincial'. A metropolis remains a metropolis in power and influence whatever the ideas which predominate in it; a province remains a province.

In Asia, Japan is such a power centre. The way Japan goes will have a profound effect on world history. Whether as a society with liberal institutions and associated with the free world, or as a neutralist country, or as a communist state, Japan is likely to be a force to be reckoned with. Were communism to be established there, Japan's policies, eventually if not immediately, would be its own policies. Japanese interests would break through the overlay of the cosmopolitan interests of communism. Moreover, Japan has the strategic position, and is able to build up sufficient force, to enable it to act by its own lights. A communist Japan would set itself aims which would be private to Japan rather than public to all communism. In this respect, it would be very different from any country in south-east Asia. No nation in this area, not even Indonesia with its immense population, would be qualified to set up as an independent communist power, evolve its own policy, or have the temerity to produce its own prophets. This difference between Japan and the countries of south-east Asia may be highly important in the next fifty years.

The communist campaign to expand will probably continue during our generation. Certainly we have not seen the end of the diverse patterns it takes. There is so much to watch, and the scene is so diverse and quick-changing, that the simple outline of what is happening is not always apparent. But beneath the turmoil and complicated interaction of events, the old divisions, the old basic interests which are a fundamental part of international politics, exercise their steady, unremitting pull. This is the explanation of the dramatic and assertive role of China in recent years.

Appendix

THE SOVIET NETWORK IN THE 'TWENTIES

IN the first years after the Russian revolution, many Russian communists were biased against activity in Asia because marxist theory prophesied that world revolution would start only in the highly industrialised countries of the West. Nevertheless, they recognised that communist movements in Asia would be useful because they would strike at the capitalist powers through their colonies. To do this was the main task of the conspiratorial organisation created in the 'twenties.

In making the network, the Russian communists knew that they had an asset in the Trans-Caucasian and Central Asian republics. As early as November 1918, Stalin, in a speech to muslim communists in Moscow, said:

> No one can erect a bridge between the East and West as quickly and easily as you can. This is because a door is opened for you to Persia, India, Afghanistan and China.

Nor were the muslims the only instruments. One group of communists saw great hopes in the buddhist Kalmucks of the Soviet empire. They might be a bridge to Asian buddhists. At least they might subvert Tibet and Tibet was on the way to India.

In 1920 there was set up a Permanent Council for Propaganda and Action of the Peoples of the East. Its tasks were mainly propaganda and conspiracy. From Baku the Council directed itself towards the Middle East; from Tashkent towards Central Asia; from Irkutsk towards the Far East. At Tashkent a school was opened for training Indian agents. Many Indians had arrived in Russia at this time, among them muslims who were supporters of the Khilafat movement, which Russia claimed to patronise. Stalin laid it down that propaganda in British India should be a 'primary objective'.

The Tashkent school was closed in March 1921, as the result of an undertaking in the Anglo-Soviet Agreement of 1920. But in place of it there appeared in Moscow the University for the Toilers of the East, whose task was to train both Soviet Central Asians and Asians from outside the Soviet Union. It gave a course lasting three years, part academic and part practical; about 2,000 students were trained there, drawn from sixty nationalities. English was the language of instruction. It was later reconstructed as the Sun Yat-sen University. In addition, there was the Lenin University, about half of whose students were Asian.

Outside Russia, the Comintern set up a Far East Bureau in Shanghai. The Women's Section of the Comintern, which was founded in 1924, specialised in propaganda to Asian women; there were active centres at Peking, Shanghai and Canton. In Shanghai there were also the headquarters of the Pan-Pacific Trade Union Congress. From these directing agencies in China, efforts were made to spread the network to south-east Asia. The Comintern set up in Singapore in 1926 a South Sea Communist Group, from which sprang the formation of the Indochinese Communist Party and the Malayan Communist Party.

Besides these organisations which were controlled ultimately by Moscow, the communist parties in the homelands of the imperialist country often thought it their right to interfere with the work of local communist groups in the colonies. From about 1925 a British Colonial Department was formed by the British Communist Party. This was criticised by communists elsewhere as being a continuation of British imperialism.

After the communist defeat in China in 1927, the network became less effective. Russia became preoccupied with Europe. For some years the communist organisations ceased to be propelled vigorously by Moscow. One reason was that some of Russia's most skilled Asian experts had opposed Stalin's view on Asia. They disappeared.

When Moscow resumed its Asian activities after the second world war, it again created an elaborate network. But the emphasis this time was on 'front organisations': organisations which claimed to be non-party and which gained wide support from left wing groups (and even from right wing eccentrics) but which in fact were under communist direction. A ramification of these now exists throughout Asia. Amongst the most active are the Asia Solidarity Committees, which aim at attracting the left wing intelligentsia, especially politicians, students and literary men. Great expectations among communists were aroused by the organisation created by the Afro-Asian Peoples Conference at Cairo in December 1957.

But the whole world-picture has been changed as the result of the Sino-Soviet quarrel. The 'front organisations' are a major prize in the struggle. Every one of the sessions of these organisations is now the scene of a 'floor-fight' between Russian and Chinese representatives. Because the Russians stand in the way of a Chinese take-over of such organisations, Peking threatens to establish its own. In the same way, China is bent on driving Russia from its patronage of the small Asian countries, and denies the Soviet Union's credentials as an Asian power entitled to participate in the next congress of Afro-Asian states. What happens at this conference will be one of the highlights of 1965.

NOTES

CHAPTER ONE

1. K. M. Panikkar, *Asia and Western Dominance* (London: George Allen & Unwin, 1953), p. 253.

CHAPTER TWO

1. The similarities between the early stages of the CCP's history and that of other Asian Communist parties are studied very suggestively in Lucian Pye, *Guerrilla Communism in Malaya* (Princeton, N. J.: Princeton University Press; London: Oxford University Press, 1956).
2. Robert North, *Moscow and Chinese Communists* (2d ed.; Stanford, Calif.: Stanford University Press; London: Oxford University Press, 1963).
3. *Ibid.*, pp. 104–5.

CHAPTER THREE

1. Siao-yu, *Mao Tse-tung and I Were Beggers* (Syracuse, N. Y.: Syracuse University Press, 1959; London: Hutchinson & Co., 1961), pp. 152–54.
2. Stuart R. Schram, *The Political Thought of Mao Tse-tung* (New York: Frederick A. Praeger; London: Pall Mall Press, 1963), p. 62.
3. Conrad Brandt, Benjamin Schwartz, and J. K. Fairbank, *A Documentary History of Chinese Communism* (Cambridge, Mass.: Harvard University Press; London: George Allen & Unwin, 1952); Mao's Hunan Agrarian Report is dealt with in full on pp. 77–89.
4. Mao Tse-tung, *Strategic Problems in the Anti-Japanese Guerrilla War* (Peking: Foreign Languages Press, 1952).
5. Cf. Mao Tse-tung, *On New Democracy* (Peking: Foreign Languages Press, 1954), pp. 17–18, 22–23.
6. Speech cited in the *Manchester Guardian,* October 29, 1956, based on monitored radio report.
7. Cf. chapters 1 and 7 of Mao's *Yu Chi Chan* (1937), translated and edited by Samuel B. Griffith as *Mao Tse-tung on Guerrilla Warfare* (New York: Frederick A. Praeger, 1961); published in Great Britain under the title *Guerrilla Warfare* (London: Cassell and Company, 1962).

CHAPTER FOUR

1. Zahir Ahmed, *Dusk and Dawn in an Indian Village* (to be published in 1965 by Frederick A. Praeger, New York, and Pall Mall Press, London).
2. *Ibid.*
3. Information given to the author.

NOTES

4. Liu Shao-chi, opening address to the Trade Union Conference of Asian and Australasian Countries, November 25, 1949.
5. Editorial in *Communist* (Bombay), II, No. 4 (1949).
6. *Izvestia Akademi Nauk ss. Serujalstorii i Filosofii* (Moscow), IX, No. 1 (1952).

CHAPTER SIX

1. David Floyd, *Mao Against Khrushchev: A Short History of the Sino-Soviet Conflict* (New York: Frederick A. Praeger; London: Pall Mall Press, 1964), p. 13.

READING LIST

The literature on the communist revolution in Asia is immense. The following books are among the most useful in the field, but the list is by no means exhaustive.

COMMUNISM IN CHINA

BARNETT, A. DOAK. *Communist China in Perspective.* New York: Frederick A. Praeger; London: Pall Mall Press, 1962.

BEAUVOIR, SIMONE DE. *The Long March.* Cleveland, Ohio: World Publishing Co.; London: André Deutsch, with Weidenfeld & Nicolson, 1958.

BOYD, R. G. *Communist China's Foreign Policy.* New York: Frederick A. Praeger; London: Pall Mall Press, 1962.

BRANDT, CONRAD, SCHWARTZ, BENJAMIN, and FAIRBANK, J. K. *A Documentary History of Chinese Communism.* Cambridge, Mass.: Harvard University Press; London: George Allen & Unwin, 1952.

CROOK, DAVID and ISABEL. *Revolution in a Chinese Village.* New York: Humanities Press; London: Routledge & Kegan Paul, 1959.

DORR, DONA (ed.). *Marx on China.* London: Lawrence and Wishart, 1951.

FITZGERALD, C. P. *Flood Tide in China.* Chester Springs, Pa.: Dufour Editions; London: Cresset Press, 1958.

ISAACS, HAROLD R. *The Tragedy of the Chinese Revolution.* Rev. ed. Stanford, Calif.: Stanford University Press, 1961.

KUO, PING-CHIA. *China: New Age and New Outlook.* New York: Alfred A. Knopf; London: Victor Gollancz, 1956.

MACFARQUHAR, RODERICK. *The Hundred Flowers Campaign and the Chinese Intellectuals.* New York: Frederick A. Praeger; London: Stevens & Sons, 1960.

MAO TSE-TUNG. *Selected Works.* 5 vols. New York: International Publishers; London: Lawrence and Wishart.

PALOCZI-HORVATH, GEORGE. *Mao Tse-tung: Emperor of the Blue Ants.* London: Secker & Warburg, 1962; New York: Doubleday & Co., 1963.

PANIKKAR, K. M. *In Two Chinas.* London: George Allen & Unwin, 1955.

ROY, M. N. *Revolution and Counter-Revolution in China.* Calcutta: Renaissance Publishers, 1946.

SCHRAM, STUART R. *The Political Thought of Mao Tse-tung.* New York: Frederick A. Praeger; London: Pall Mall Press, 1963.

SCHWARTZ, BENJAMIN. *Chinese Communism and the Rise of Mao.* Cambridge, Mass.: Harvard University Press; London: Oxford University Press, 1951.

SMEDLEY, AGNES. *The Great Road: The Life and Times of Chu Teh.* New York: Monthly Review Press; London: John Calder, 1958.

SNOW, EDGAR. *The Other Side of the River: Red China Today.* New York: Random House, 1962; London: Victor Gollancz, 1963.

———. *Red Star Over China.* New ed. Gloucester, Mass.: Peter Smith; London: Victor Gollancz, 1964.

TROTSKY, LEON. *Problems of the Chinese Revolution.* 2d ed. San Francisco: Paragon Publications, 1962.

COMMUNISM IN ASIA

BARNETT, A. DOAK (ed.). *Communist Strategies in Asia.* New York: Frederick A. Praeger; London: Pall Mall Press, 1963.

BELOFF, MAX. *Soviet Policy in the Far East, 1944–1951.* London and New York: Oxford University Press, 1953.

BRACKMAN, ARNOLD C. *Indonesian Communism: A History.* New York and London: Frederick A. Praeger, 1963.

BRIMMELL, J. H. *Communism in South-east Asia.* London and New York: Oxford University Press, 1959.

COLBERT, EVELYN. *The Left Wing in Japanese Politics.* Vancouver: Institute of Pacific Relations, 1952.

FALL, BERNARD B. *The Two Viet-Nams.* Rev. ed. New York: Frederick A. Praeger; London: Pall Mall Press, 1964.

GIAP, VO NGUYÊN. *People's War, People's Army: The Viet Công Insurrection Manual for Underdeveloped Countries.* New York and London: Frederick A. Praeger, 1962.

HOANG VAN CHI. *From Colonialism to Communism: A Case History of North Vietnam.* New York: Frederick A. Praeger; London: Pall Mall Press, 1964.

HONEY, P. J. *Communism in North Vietnam.* Cambridge, Mass.: The M.I.T. Press, 1963.

KENNEDY, MALCOLM. *A Short History of Communism in Asia.* London: Weidenfeld & Nicolson, 1956. Published in the United States under the title *A History of Communism in East Asia.* New York: Frederick A. Praeger, 1957.

LAQUEUR, WALTER. *Communism and Nationalism in the Middle East.* 2d ed. New York: Frederick A. Praeger; London: Routledge & Kegan Paul, 1957.

MICHAEL, FRANZ H., and TAYLOR, GEORGE E. *The Far East in the Modern World.* New York: Henry Holt and Co.; London: Methuen & Co., 1956.

PYE, LUCIAN. *Guerrilla Communism in Malaya.* Princeton, N.J.: Princeton University Press; London: Oxford University Press, 1956.

SWEARINGEN, RODGER, and LANGER, PAUL F. *Red Flag in Japan.* Cambridge, Mass.: Harvard University Press, 1952.

TRUONG CHINH. *Primer for Revolt: The Communist Takeover in Vietnam.* New York and London: Frederick A. Praeger, 1963.

SINO-INDIAN RELATIONS

FISHER, MARGARET W., ROSE, LEO E., and HUTTENBACK, ROBERT A. *Himalayan Battleground: Sino-Indian Rivalry in Ladakh.* New York: Frederick A. Praeger; London: Pall Mall Press, 1963.

KARNIK, V. B. *China Invades India.* Bombay: Allied Publishers, 1963.

LAMB, ALASTAIR. *The China-India Border.* London and New York: Oxford University Press, 1964.

PATTERSON, GEORGE N. *Peking Versus Delhi.* New York: Frederick A. Praeger; London: Faber & Faber, 1964.

SPRATT, PHILIP. *Blowing-up India.* Calcutta: Prachi Prakashan, 1955.

SINO-SOVIET RELATIONS

FLOYD, DAVID. *Mao Against Khrushchev: A Short History of the Sino-Soviet Conflict.* New York: Frederick A. Praeger; London: Pall Mall Press, 1964.

MEHNERT, KLAUS. *Peking and Moscow.* New York: G. P. Putnam's Sons; London: Weidenfeld & Nicolson, 1963.

NORTH, ROBERT. *Moscow and Chinese Communists.* 2d ed. Stanford, Calif.: Stanford University Press; London: Oxford University Press, 1963.

WU, AITCHEN. *China and the Soviet Union.* London: Methuen & Co., 1950.

ZAGORIA, DONALD S. *The Sino-Soviet Conflict, 1956–1961.* Princeton, N.J.: Princeton University Press, 1962.

INDEX

ACADEMY of Red Professors, 10
Afghanistan, 102, 125
Afro-Asian Conference 1957, 127
Albania, 111, 113
All Men Are Brothers, 32
Andhra rebellion, 56
Anglo-Soviet Agreement, 1920, 126
Anti-Fascist Peoples Freedom League, 53
Asian Communism, 2, 28; early plans and prospects, 4-11; post-1945, first phase, 47, 48-54; 2nd phase, 55-61; 3rd phase, 61-6. (See also under individual countries.)
Asian network, Russian, 10, 125-7
Asian Solidarity Committee, 127

BAKU, 126
Bandung Conference, Era, 81, 82, 92, 98
Belgian CP, 107
Bengal, 57
Berlin blockade, 55
Bokhara, khanate of, 7
Bolshevist, -ism, 3, 15, 17, 18, 20
Border Question, Sino-Russian, 104
Border War, Sino-Indian, 86n; Chinese case, 93-4; Nehru-Chou 1954 meeting, 95; history of border, 95-6; 1960 Indian mission, 97; Chinese motives, 97-100; India worsted, 100; and isolated in Asia, 101; effect on Indian CP, 101
Borneo, 118
Borodin, Michael, 2, 20, 23
Bose, Subhas, 48
Britain, British, 53, 56, 57, 59, 63, 75, 76 and n, 94, 98, 99, 100, 101, 105; British Communist Party, 63, 108, 127
Buddhism, -ists, 29, 79n, 82, 92, 119, 125-6
Bukharin, N. I., 22
Bulganin, N., 85
Burma, 55, 119; Burmese communism, 52, 53, 54; insurgency, 56, 59-60; and China, 73, 101

CAIRO, conference at, 127
Calcutta, 57; Youth Congress at, 55, 63
Cambodia, 117n
Canton, 17, 24, 126
CENTO, 114
Ceylon, 48
Chang-Sha, 30
Chiang Kai-shek, 24, 25, 40, 42, 43, 68, 69, 86, 118, 119
Chinghiz Khan, 34
China, Imperial, and Republic of, 5, 17, 18, 23, 43, 76 and n, 93n, 95-6, 104
China, People's Republic of, 25, 45, 87, 93; aims and policy of, 67, 68, 71, 79, 80, 86-7, 88-9, 90-1, 97-100, 104, 109-12, 113-14, 117, 119 and n, 120; and Africa, 3, 90, 110, 111-12, 120-1; and Asia, 62, 68-9, 71, 73-4, 78, 81, 90, 92, 93, 98-9, 100, 101, 104, 111, 113-15, 119, 123; and Latin America, 3, 62, 90; and Middle East, 62, 110, 112, 121; and Tibet, 75, 76-7 and n, 92-3, 95-8; and European communist parties, 107-8, 111; traditionalism of, 68, 73, 79n, 93n, 97, 110. (See also *Border Question, Border War, Sino-Indian* and *Sino-Russian Relations*.)
Chinese Communism: See under *China, Chinese Communist Party,* and *Mao Tse-tung*
Chinese Communist Party (CCP), 2, 12, 13, 19, 29, 34; early history of, 17-18; in 1930s, 37-8, 40, 42; in Sino-Japanese war, 42-3; conquers China, 44; CCP and Kuomintang, 2, 24, 25, 43; and Indian CP, 62-4; and CPSU, 16-17, 65, 105; and Stalin, 2, 23, 25; central committee of, 35, 39, 40; 8th congress of, 40
Chou En-lai, 24, 25, 79-80, 81, 90, 95, 111-12, 114
Chu-teh, 43
Chungking, 43
Coexistence, peaceful, 90

Cominform, 64
Comintern, 11, 17, 22, 25, 37; Far East Bureau, 9, 126; Chinese Sub-committee, 22-3
Commandism, 89
Communist, 64
Congo, 121
Confucius, 32
Cuba, 85, 110, 113
Czechoslovakia, 55

Dalai lama, 76, 78n, 93
De Gaulle, 33, 119-20
Dostoievsky, 11
Dulles, John Foster, 80
Dutch, 53, 60

East turkestan, Republic of, 70
Engels, 63, 113

Fall, Bernard B., 116n
Floyd, David, 105n
Formosa (Taiwan), 44, 69, 86, 113, 118
France, French, 6, 53, 61, 78n, 115, 119; French CP, 107
Fukien, Chinese soviet in, 26, 27

Gandhi, 34, 80
Geneva Agreement, 115, 117
Germany, 9, 48, 78n
Glory of the Hans, 33
'Great Leap Forward', 88-90, 111

Han people, 110
Harriman, Averell, 45
Hitler, 2, 78n
Ho Chi Minh, 115-16 and n
Hukbalahaps, 54, 56
Hunan, 25, 29, 30, 34-5
Hungary, 85
Hyderabad, 57

India, 48, 60, 103, 125, 126; and Asia, 77, 80-1, 100; and Russia, 97, 99, 103; and Tibet, 75, 76-8, 81-2, 93; Congress party, government, 52, 56; insurgence in, 57-9. (See also Border War and Sino-Indian Relations.)
Indian Communist Party, 52, 54, 56-9, 62-4, 97, 101, 111

Indochina, communism in, 52, 53, 56, 61, 112, 115, 126. (See also Vietnam.)
Indonesia, 115, 118, 124; and China, 73, 113, 115; insurgence in, 56, 59, 60
Indonesian Communist Party, 12, 49, 52, 53-4, 61, 118
International Commission of Jurists, 78n
Ireland, 78
Irkutsk, Far East Centre at, 126
Islam, see under Muslims
Italian Communist Party, 107-8

Japan, Japanese, 10 and n, 18, 43, 45, 47-8, 53, 54, 123-4; and China, 113
Japanese Communist Party, 49, 74-5
Joint Pacific Fleet, Sino-Soviet, 85, 87

Kalmucks, 125
Kanpus (cadres), 71
Kashmir, 96, 102
Khams, revolt of, 92
Khilafat movement, 126
Khiva, khanate of, 7
Khrushchev, N. S., 73, 85, 86, 90, 106-9
Kiangsi, Chinese soviet in, 26, 27, 37, 39-40
Kim Il-sung, 73
Korea: North, 71, 72, 73-4; South, 71, 72, 73
Korean War, 62, 71-3, 75, 79, 89, 110
Kuo, P. C., 31 and n
Kuomintang, 2, 10, 18-20, 39, 42, 54, 69, 86; gains control, 24; breach with communists, 25; in Sino-Japanese war, 43-4; collapse and defeat of, 44; and Stalin, 21, 23, 42, 70

Ladakh, 95, 96, 97
Land Reform, 110-11
Laqueur, Walter, 45
League for the Liberation of the East, 10
League Against Imperialism, 10
Lenin, 2 and n, 14, 16, 29, 33, 36, 46, 63, 113; and China, 20
Lenin University, 10, 126
Liu Shao-chi, 62, 63
Liberalism, 5

Li Li-san, 41-2
Long March, The, 27, 38, 40

MACMAHON, Sir Henry, 95
MacMahon Line, 95, 96
Magsaysay, Ramón, 60
Malaya, 115; insurgency in, 38, 52, 56, 59, 60; and China, 115
Malayan Communist Party, 53, 60-1, 122
Malaysia, 118, 119
Manchu dynasty, 5, 18
Manchuria, 38n, 43, 70, 71
Mao Tse-tung, 2, 28, 57, 59, 61, 65, 70, 86, 119; early life, 29-30; early role in CCP, 34-5, 37, 39; victory of, 44; status in communist world, 84, 109, 113, 115-16; and Chinese national character, 31-3; and marxism, 29, 30-2, 33, 34, 39n, 45, 84-5; on revolution, 32-3, 35-7, 45; on 'New Democracy', 38-9 and n; military tactics of, 36, 37, 43
Marshall, General, 44
Marx, 6, 31, 32, 63, 113
Marxism and the National Question, 77
Mencius, 32
Middle East, communism in, 45, 62; Baku centre for communism in, 126
Mongol people, 94
Mongolia: Inner, 70; Outer, 7, 38, 70, 104-5
Mongolian Communist Party, 105
Muslims, 9, 82, 125, 126
Mussolini, 118

NATIONALISM and communism, 8, 9, 19, 20, 44, 45, 53-4, 56, 71, 77, 113-14
Nehru, Jawarhalal, 77, 80, 81, 92, 95, 99, 101, 102
Nepal, 101
'New Democracy', 38-9, 63
Non-alignment, 80, 81, 100
North, Richard, 22
Northern Expedition, 24, 54
North-East Frontier Agency, 95
Nosaka, S., 74
Noulens case, 10
Nuclear arms, war, 86, 87, 88, 90, 91, 105, 108, 109
Nyerere, Julius, 121

PAKISTAN, 48, 102; and China, 101
Panch Sheela, 81-2, 92
Pan-Pacific Trades Union Secretariat, 10, 126
Panikkar, K. M., 11, 77
Peasantry, revolutionary, military role of, 15-16, 20, 21n, 31-2, 33-4, 35-7, 44, 61, 110
Peng Te-huai, 87-8
Peasant Unions, 22, 23, 34
People's Communes, 88, 89, 111
People's Democratic Front, 54
People's Liberation Movement, 46
Permanent Council for Propaganda and Action, 126
Persia, 125
Philippines, 113, 115; insurgency in, 54, 56, 59, 60; and China, 113
Poland, 6, 85
Port Arthur, 85

QUEMOY and Matsu, 86, 86n

RADEK, K. B., 10
Ranadive, B. T., 89; attack on Mao, 63-4
Red Army: Russian, 6; Chinese, 59, 73, 99, 103
Report on . . . the Agrarian Movement in Hunan, 35
Revisionism, 90, 112
Revolution, communist theories of: 'armed rev.', 23; Middle East rev., 45; Moscow theories, 7, 11, 15-16, 21-3, 65; Peking theories, 31-4, 35-7, 38-9 and n, 44, 62, 63, 90-1, 110, 111-12. (See also *Mao Tse-tung* and *Peasantry*.)
Roy, M. N., 10, 25
Russia, Tsarist, 5, 6-7, 11, 13, 16, 17, 47, 104
Russia, Soviet, 67-8, 70, 71-2, 122; and Asia, 2, 5, 7, 47, 49, 54-5, 63, 97, 104, 125-9; and India, 97, 99, 103; and muslim world, 9, 125-6. (See also *Border Question*, *Sino-Russian Relations* and *Soviet Communist Party*.)
Russian aid to China, 45, 70-1, 85, 86 and n, 88

SAN CHI MIN I, 19
San Salvador, 78

Schram, Stuart, 33
SEATO, 114, and n, 117
Security Council, 120
Shanghai, 17, 24; communist centre in, 9, 10, 39, 126
Shensi, 38
Siao-yu, 30
Siberia, 104, 106
Sihanouk, Prince, 117n
Simla Conference, Treaty of, 95, 96
Singapore, communism in, 10, 53, 126
Sinkiang, 96, 104
Sino-Japanese War, 38, 43
Sino-Indian relations, 75-82, 86n, 92, 93-102, 111
Sino-Russian relations, 1-2, 6, 14, 17, 19, 20-1, 38, 42, 45-6, 63, 65, 67, 70-1, 73, 83-91, 97-8, 101, 103-5, 108-9, 112, 120, 127. (See also Border Question.)
Sjarifuddin, Amir, 54
Socialism, 39, 85, 114, 116
Somalia, 121
Sorge, Richard, 10 and n
South Seas Communist Group, 10, 126
Soviet Communist Party (CPSU), 16, 19, 68, 90, 111; and Chinese Communist Party, 65, 107, 109
Soviet Union: see Russia, Soviet
Spanish Civil War, 38
Stalin, 2, 10, 25, 46, 63, 101, 113; and Asia, 49, 125-6; and Chinese communism, 2, 23, 25, 45, 70, 84; and Kuomintang, 21, 23, 42, 70; and Korean war, 72; on nationalism, 52; on revolution, 21-3
Sukarno, 118
Sun Yat-sen, 18, 19
Sun Yat-sen University, 10, 126

TAIPING, rebellion, 37
Tanganyika and Zanzibar, United Republic of, 121

Tashkent, communist centre at, 126
Telingana, revolt in, 57-9
Test-ban treaty, 105-6
Thailand, 115; and China, 113
Theses on the National and Colonial Question, 16
Tibet, 75-8, 80, 81, 82, 92-3, 95-6, 97-8, 125
Timur, 34
Tito, 85, 90
Togliatti, Palmiro, 22, 108
Tokuda, K., 74
Treint, R., 22
Trotsky, 44, 72
Truman, President, 44, 72

U NU, 55
United Nations, 72, 78, 79, 119-20
University of the Toilers of the East, 10, 126
United States, 68-70, 71, 72, 73, 74, 75, 79, 80, 86, 100, 103, 105, 113, 114, 115, 117 and n, 118; and recognition of China, 69-70, 119-20
US Seventh Fleet, 118

VIET MINH, 53, 59, 115
Vietnam, 53, 109; North, 115, 116, 117n; South, 116, 117 and n; 119

WANG CHING-WEI, 25
Whampoa Military Academy, 24, 25, 121
World Federation of Trade Unions, 54

YANGTZE valley, 24, 25, 27, 37
Yenan, 43

ZANZIBAR, 113, 121
Zhdanov, A. A., 55, 66
Zhukov, Marshal, 63